making the mummies dance

Would-be Preachers Delivering Life-Giving Sermons

CHRIS SPICER

malcolm down
PUBLISHING

First published in 2021 by Malcolm Down Publishing Ltd.
www.malcolmdown.co.uk

British Library Cataloguing in Publication Data
A catalogue record for this book is available from the British Library.

ISBN 978-1-912863-82-2

Design by Esther Kotecha
Cover photography by Paul Lapsley

Printed in the UK

BY THE SAME AUTHOR

No Perfect Fathers Here
JJ & the Big Bend
The Reel Story
Life on the Hill

DEDICATION

This book is dedicated to all those would-be preachers who will yet *Make the Mummies Dance!*

CONTENTS

Acknowledgements 9
Introduction 11
1. Take the Call 19
2. Be Yourself 37
3. Find Your Voice 55
4. Create a Pearl 75
5. Move Beyond the Margin 91
6. Make an Investment 107
7. Bait the Hook 125
8. Enjoy the Journey 143
9. Feel the Burn 159
10. Order a Takeaway 177
Conclusion 195
Appendix 201
About the Author 207
Recommended Resources 208

ACKNOWLEDGEMENTS

Looking back over fifty years of preaching and teaching there are so many people who have mentored me in the art of proclaiming God's Word – to those I simply say thank you. Also a big shout out to Tim Cross, Roger Blackmore, Terry Bennett and Paul Finn who gave me excellent feedback on the original manuscript. I would also like to thank Mark Stibbe for his editorial help, Esther Kotecha for her cover design and internal layout, Paul Lapsley for the cover photography and Louise Stenhouse for her expertise in proofreading. And last, but by no means least, my wife Tina whose constant companionship through half a century of journeying together, has made all of this possible.

INTRODUCTION

The problem with writing a book on any subject is that people immediately think you are an expert. In my case, nothing could be further from the truth. If proof is required, you only need to hear about my first cringeworthy attempt at preaching.

I was about to enter Bible college and the local church leadership, in their infinite wisdom, decided to give me the opportunity to preach. With no training and only my personal observations of others to fall back on, I took the safe option by preaching from John's Gospel, chapter 3, and verse 16. In those days, the preferred Bible translation was the King James Version: *For God so loved the world, that he gave his only begotten Son, that whosoever believeth in him should not perish, but have everlasting life.*

Even though I was allocated twenty minutes, my homily lasted ten agonising minutes. Stepping away from the pulpit, I vowed never to preach again – strange when you consider that fifty years on I am still preaching and teaching God's Word.

Having regained some level of composure, I asked a *critical friend*[1] for some constructive feedback. Having first softened me up with a few encouraging words, he moved in to deliver the knockout blow. It appears that my nerves had gotten the better of me. Every time I had intended to use the word *"begotten"*, I had inadvertently used the word *"forgotten"*. I had unwittingly preached the world's first sermon on "God's Only Forgotten Son"!

So, why write a book on preachers and preaching? The answer is twofold. Firstly, having been asked on numerous occasions to share my thoughts on the subject, I decided to put pen to paper. Believing the best preachers are yet to come, my hope is that these writings will kickstart a conversation and help to provide some clear guidance.

Secondly, my assessment of 21st-century preaching, although not totally dismissive, is that many preachers are in dire need of help. Apart from a few pockets of resistance, much of what goes under the guise of preaching is sadly nothing more than the bland leading the bland – horrible snore-inducing sermons,[2] condescending chats, tiresome imitation TED Talks for which the only redeeming factor is their brevity.

In some charismatic settings, preaching has become the poor-relation of praise and worship. Corporate worship is intended to build a platform for the proclamation of God's Word, and yet preaching has become an afterthought, the closing remarks in a religious event we call "church". In an age when Christians are worshipping worship, true biblical preaching is in need of a radical rethink.

I would go further. Now is the time for a renaissance in preachers and preaching. So how do we take that which has the potential to give life and make it live? How do we do

---

[1] "Critical Friend . . . is someone who is encouraging and supportive, but who also provides honest and often candid feedback that may be uncomfortable or difficult to hear . . . someone who agrees to speak truthfully, but constructively, about weaknesses, problems, and emotionally charged issues" www.edglossary.org. All would-be preachers need "Critical Friends".

this thing called preaching better?

Making the Mummies Dance

This is a sketchbook on the art of preaching. I don't expect everyone to appreciate these scribblings, but I do humbly offer them as helpful hints for those called to communicate biblical truth in a post-Christian world.

Having spent half a century speaking in homes, churches, and training institutions, I have, through the medium of radio, television, and the internet, had to prepare numerous talks for a variety of listeners. I don't say this to boast; I give all the glory to God that this shy, uneducated, introverted individual has, over time, proved that *God deliberately chose men and women that the culture overlooks and exploits and abuses, chose these "nobodies" to expose the hollow pretensions of "somebodies" . . . That makes it quite clear that none of you can get by with blowing your own horn before God.*[3] Time has taught me that preaching is more than instructing others. It is about the transformation of lives. For that to happen, God must be the inspiration before, during and after every preaching event.

True biblical preaching generates a life-giving atmosphere. No matter the background, culture, age, or level of understanding of the listener, preachers are agents of change. Partnering with the Holy Spirit, preachers are compassionate individuals who live and die for the transformation of other people's lives.

---

2 Throughout *Making the Mummies Dance* we will use the terms "messages", "sermons", "talks" and "homilies" interchangeably.

3 1 Corinthians 1:28, MSG

In the 1960s, Thomas Hoving was the Commissioner of Parks for the City of New York. Having a PhD in art history from Princeton, he was somewhat ill-placed in the administration of Mayor John Lindsay. But everything was about to change. Hoving was approached by the Board of The Metropolitan Museum of Art to become their director. For someone with a PhD in art history, to be offered the role of director in this prestigious art museum was a no-brainer. Hoving jumped at the chance!

Having only served for a few months as Commissioner of Parks, Thomas Hoving would have to discuss his decision with Mayor Lindsay. Concerned about the response, he somewhat reluctantly made his way to Lindsay's office.

"I've been offered the role of director of The Metropolitan Museum of Art," he said, "and I'd like to take it."

He then waited for the Mayor's response.

"Well, it's a great opportunity," Lindsay replied. "But have you considered the boredom? Seems to me the place is dead. Having said that, you'll **make the mummies dance**!"[4] What a phrase!

Preaching Properly

If we do this thing called preaching properly, we should aim to make the mummies dance. We should take that which has the potential to bring death[5] and make it live. With God's help, we can take words, phrases and doctrines that seem heavy and soporific and breathe life into them. We can see spiritual mausoleums turned into maternity wards full of

---

[4] Thomas Hoving, *Making the Mummies Dance* (Simon & Schuster, 1993)

[5] 2 Corinthians 3:6

new birth. We can see listeners who are spiritually dead and dying stand up and bear witness to the resurrection life of Jesus Christ. If only we do this thing called preaching correctly. So, come with me on a journey of discovery and learn what it means:

- To breathe life into biblical truth
- To bring vitality to those mummified places and people where we have the opportunity to minister God's Word
- To take the spark of an idea and craft it into a life-changing sermon
- To come up with words and explore themes in the great task of communicating biblical truth to a post-Christian culture
- To unashamedly be our true self and recognise our signature sound
- To preach prophetically as a seer and as a spokesperson of the unseen
- To preach in a priestly manner to connect people with a loving heavenly Father

Not All Preaching is Preaching

"What we call preaching, the formal public address to the gathered congregation on a Sunday, is only one form of what the Bible describes as 'ministry of the Word' (Acts 6:2, 6:4)."[6] The idea that every Christian should be able

---

6 Peter Adam, *Speaking God's Words: A Practical Theology of Preaching* (Vancouver, British Columbia: Regent College Publishing, 1996), p. 59

to preach in a formal public gathering is not only short-sighted but a misunderstanding of what the Bible teaches. In Acts 8:4, when persecution caused the church to scatter leaving the leaders in Jerusalem, we learn *those who had been scattered went about* ***preaching the word.*** The next verse says, *Philip went down to the city of Samaria and began* ***proclaiming Christ to them.***[7] In both instances the word "preach" is used. However, in the first a better translation would be that the believers were gossiping the gospel in the manner encouraged by 1 Peter 3:15 – *always [be] ready to make a defence to everyone who asks you to give an account for the hope that is in you.*[8] In the second, the word used of Philip means to "herald" or "preach" the gospel. The same writer (Luke) therefore makes a distinction between two different kinds of utterance. Every Christ follower should be ready to gossip the gospel, but not all are called to do what Phillip did.

In his excellent book *Preaching: Communicating Faith in an Age of Scepticism*, Timothy Keller reminds us that the New Testament word translated "preaching" or "proclaiming" can be divided into three different activities.

- **Type 1** – The informal conversational ministering of God's Word on a one-to-one basis, something every Christian should be able to do. This act of gossiping the gospel is what the apostle Paul was considering when writing to the Christians in Colossae saying, *Let the word of Christ dwell in you richly, teaching and admonishing one another in all wisdom.*[9]

---

[7] Acts 8:4–5, NASB
[8] 1 Peter 3:15, NASB
[9] Colossians 3:16, ESV

- **Type 2** – This lies between the *informal* type 1 and more *formal* type 3 preaching. Keller links this with the *gift of speaking*.[10] This "includes personal exhortation or counselling, evangelism, and teaching individuals and groups". He also includes those gifted with the skills of "writing, blogging, song writing, poetry, teaching classes and small groups, mentoring, moderating open discussion forums on issues of faith, and so on".[11]

- **Type 3** – This is what is more commonly understood as proclaiming God's Word to a congregation. It is this type of preaching which will form the focus of *Making the Mummies Dance*. However, it is my belief that we are about to see a much-needed renaissance in all three types of proclaiming God's truth.

Please, therefore, remember that there is a variety of utterances implied by the word "preaching". To limit this to one type is a hinderance to the expansion of the gospel of the kingdom. The church needs to champion a multi-faceted approach to preaching, no matter a person's style or setting. The author, songwriter, poet, and blogger are no less instrumental in proclaiming God's Word than one speaking to a formal gathering on Sunday.

---

10 1 Peter 4:10-11

11 Timothy Keller, *Preaching: Communicating Faith in an Age of Scepticism* (Hodder & Stoughton, 2015).

TAKE THE CALL 1

Although this may take a quantum leap of faith to visualise, Christianity is moving towards a tipping point, a moment when the church crosses a spiritual threshold into a whole new sphere of influence. When this happens, the best churches and best preachers will begin to emerge. That may seem far away, I admit, especially while minor-league churches insist on copycatting their major-league counterparts, resulting in a concerning lack of emerging preachers. Indeed, I often find myself changing the lyrics of Pete Seegar's folksong. Replacing the word "preachers" where he sings "flowers", I hear, "Where have all the preachers gone, long time passing. Where have all the preachers gone, long time ago."

Listed in the "Top 20 Political Songs", Seegar's lyrics were used powerfully in the 1960s as part of the demonstrations against the tragic loss of young life during the Vietnam War. This song vented both the sorrow and anger over the fading flower of America's youth. My first visit to America in the mid-70s was memorable not because of the New York skyscrapers nor the vast open spaces but because of the absence of young men of my age. I mourn the loss of a generation of would-be preachers.

RATHER THAN FROM THE MILLENNIALS, THE BEST PREACHERS WILL IN ALL PROBABILITY EMERGE FROM GENERATION Z[1]

There is a great need for the current generation of young men and women to take up the baton of preaching. In this, it seems that the Millennials may also have become a lost generation. Whether it's the intimidating professionalism of some preachers or the challenge of preaching God's Word in a consumeristic age, someone or something has created an atmosphere of self-disqualification among Millennials. Maybe church leaders are at fault by setting the bar so high that would-be preachers are unable to meet such unattainable heights. I also wonder if the quick-fix stardom of TV programmes like *Britain's Got Talent, Pop Idol* and *Stars in Their Eyes* has fed an

1 The generation reaching adulthood in the second decade of the 21st Century.

entitlement generation with a false belief in instant success. While I admire those who publicly preach well, we should not forget that their journey to the present destination has been long, arduous, and at times costly.

Whatever the real reason, 21st-century Christians seem to be reluctant to take hold of the baton being held out by a generation fast coming to the end of their race.

The Call

No one can simply decide to become a preacher; they are called, commissioned, and sent by God. Speaking of those outside the Christian faith, the apostle Paul asks a pertinent question. *How are they to hear [the gospel] without someone preaching? And how are they to preach unless they are sent?*[2] As one of the 20th-century's best preachers would say at the start of his homiletics class:

"Without the call, no course can help you be a good preacher. You need to know you're sent, commissioned, that [God is] with you . . . I cannot give you what God has not given you, nor train you in

HEAVEN IS PUTTING OUT A CALL TO VARIOUS PEOPLE TO PROCLAIM GOD'S WORD. THE QUESTION IS, WHO WILL HEAR AND OBEY?

[2] Romans 10:14,15, ESV

what is not there. You must have a 'burning within' to proclaim."[3]

Preachers do what they do from an awareness of a divine calling. Paraphrasing the opening verses of Jeremiah, the person who is called to preach hears these words deep within their soul: *Before you were born I appointed you as a preacher.*[4] This statement causes us to ask, "What is the call? How is it best defined?" The best answer I can give to these questions is to reflect on my personal experience and tell you my story.

PREACHING IS NOT SOMETHING WE DECIDE TO DO; IT IS SOMETHING WE HAVE TO DO

Some preachers experience the immediacy of a "Damascus Road" type call.[5] Blinded by the brilliance of the glorified, risen Christ, they are supernaturally knocked off their high horse of self-importance. Like Saul, these individuals experience a divine encounter that leaves them questioning the source of this overwhelming power and the purpose for which heaven has arrested them.[6] In my case, however, the call was more gradual. Over an extended period, I became aware that God was up to something.

This was a pivotal moment in my life characterised by three things: a

3 Bryn Jones, *Introduction to Homiletics*, Seminar Study Notes
4 Jeremiah 1:5, paraphrased
5 Acts 9:1-18
6 Acts 9:1-18; Philippians 3:12

holy discontent created by a *heavenly disturbance* that caused me to make a *personal dedication* to God's will for my life.

- **Holy Discontent** – In the late 1960s, my life was at a crossroads. Before me lay two career choices. One would take me into a teacher training college; the other, which was my father's preference,[7] would have me take up the offer of a directorship in the family business. In this, I came to experience a feeling of *holy discontent*. I was at a tipping point, about to cross the threshold into something new. These feelings created a sense of urgency to seek God.

  Naturally speaking, I had everything a young twenty-something would want – great career choices, a brand-new top-of-the-range sports car, money in the bank, and options on a bachelor pad. However, these temporal and material things had lost their attraction. This was a critical moment in which God began the commissioning process. It was a time of *holy discontent* that

MY DISCONTENT COULD EITHER FRUSTRATE OR FUEL MY PASSION TO FIND AND FULFIL GOD'S PURPOSE FOR MY LIFE

[7] Although my father found it hard to understand my refusal to join a business that he had built for his two sons, the turning point came when he heard me preach a sermon in our home church on *The Great Reunion of Christ's Return*. Although naturally he struggled to understand, spiritually he had to acknowledge my call to preach.

was about to lead into a *heavenly disturbance.*

- **Heavenly Disturbance** – God was disrupting my comfort zone. *Like an eagle that stirs up its nest,*[8] He was lovingly encouraging me to launch out, to test those spiritual abilities He had woven in me in my mother's womb. The great winemaker had stepped into my life and found that I had *been at ease [undisturbed] from [my] youth.* God was turning my life around.[9] He was wrecking me for anything less than pursuing the purpose of God. In his book *Preaching and Preachers,* Dr Martyn Lloyd-Jones puts it like this: "You are certain of the call when you are unable to keep it back and to resist it. You try your utmost to do so. You say, 'No, I shall go on with what I am doing; I am able to do it and it is good work.' You do your utmost to push back and to rid yourself of *this disturbance in your spirit* which comes in these various ways. But you reach the point when you cannot do so any longer. It almost becomes an obsession, and so overwhelming that in the end

FOCUSING ON GOD'S CALL AVOIDS FATIGUE AND FRUSTRATION

[8] Deuteronomy 32:11, NASB
[9] Jeremiah 48:11

you say, 'I can do nothing else, I cannot resist any longer.'"[10]

Personally, I had reached the point of no return and I could do nothing else.

- **Personal Dedication** – Having surrendered to God's will for my life, I found myself in the place of the apostles who in Acts 6 *devoted themselves to prayer and to ministry of the Word.*[11] Having delegated a crucial ministry of providing for others, the apostles were free to *give [their] full attention to prayer and preaching of the word of God.*[12] It is only when would-be preachers give themselves fully to the task at hand that they will see *the word of God [keep] on spreading; and the number of the disciples [continue] to increase greatly*[13] in our towns and cities.

PREACHING IS NOT SOME PASTIME WE PICK UP AS AND WHEN WE PLEASE, A SPIRITUAL TOY WE ENJOY FOR A WHILE, ONLY TO DISCARD

Proclaiming God's Word is an activity in which the Holy Spirit brings heaven to earth through those called to become couriers of truth. What began as holy discontent, in a season of heavenly disturbance, culminated in a personal decision to devote my whole life to this

10 Dr Martyn Lloyd-Jones, *Preaching and Preachers,* (Hodder & Stoughton, 1971)
11 Acts 6:1-7, ESV
12 Acts 6:3-4, TPT
13 Acts 6:7, NASB

glorious call, to preach and teach God's Word.

What is often difficult to define was for me made easier when I was asked, while studying church leadership in Portland, Oregon, to write a short essay entitled, "My Awareness of Calling". Having already spent thirty years preaching and teaching God's Word, this essay, although somewhat religious in its wording and dated in its style, nevertheless outlines what happened to me when God came calling.

OUR STORY CAN BRING GOD GLORY

"Growing up in a godly environment, I fostered from an early age a desire to serve God, yet this was often overshadowed by feelings of personal inadequacy. Through prayer, godly direction and practical discipline, the Holy Spirit prepared me for service and began to *nullify the things that are, so that no one should boast before [God]* (1 Corinthians 1:28-30). Once ignited, that inner sense of purpose, although not crystallised in all its aspects, began to burn with greater intensity.

It's thirty years later now and that drive to take others by the hand and lead them in their God-given destiny still constrains me; that longing to take the bread of life and, with God's blessing, break it in into bite-sized pieces to feed the hungry, still consumes me; that passion to mine the gold of revelatory truth from the rock of God's Word, craft it through study and research, then have the eternal assayer place His stamp of anointing on it, still crowns my every desire and goal in life. Just as the wind causes a sailboat to cut a swathe through strong waves, so the sense of divine call drives me ever onward to *take hold of that for which Christ Jesus took hold of me.*[14]

IT IS THIS CALL THAT GETS ME UP IN THE MORNING AND MOTIVATES ME TO STAY ON TRACK WHEN OTHERS CONSPIRE TO DERAIL ME

I grew up listening to preachers telling me about the importance of finding your calling. I have also spoken about this principle. Sadly, it is wrong! It is based on the idea that it is we who take the initiative, we who do the finding. While there is an element of truth in this, the Bible shows that men like Samuel never tried to find their calling; their calling found them. Perhaps the greatest of the Old Testament prophets, Samuel was a class act; he served a nation that was falling apart at the seams. Yet because of his willingness to serve the purpose of

[14] Philippians 3:12

God in obscurity, God came calling with a phenomenal opportunity.

The so-called "Prince of Preachers" was Charles Haddon Spurgeon. He was a Baptist minister in London in the nineteenth century and spoke at his church, The Metropolitan Tabernacle, to up to ten thousand people at a time. Said to be the most eloquent preacher in a century, he once described the calling like this: "If you can do anything else do it. If you can stay out of the ministry, stay out of the ministry."[15]

THE CALL TO PREACH CARRIES WITH IT A SENSE OF COMPULSION, A DIVINE CONSTRAINT TO DO WHAT WE CANNOT AVOID

God-given Authority

One of the notable characteristics of the preaching and teaching of Jesus was that He spoke *as one who had authority.*[16] He spoke as someone with a God-given legal right to speak. That marked Him out as different from the religious teachers of His day. "He was creative, direct, compassionate, and offensive. He was the master communicator. People who were nothing like Him, liked Him. Sinners and tax gatherers flocked to hear Him."[17]

Think of someone in authority and you'll probably imagine a police

15 Dr Martyn Lloyd-Jones, *Preaching and Preachers,* p. 105
16 Matthew 7:29
17 Andy Stanley and Lane Jones, *Communicating for a Change* (Multnomah Books, 2006)

officer – someone who has the legal right to act in accordance with the law. If requested, we stop what we are doing and obey their words. This same sense of authority is contained within the words of someone called to preach, only this time we are talking about spiritual authority. Without this authority, people are merely secular communicators. We might find them captivating and interesting, but they lack the spiritual impetus to bring godly change.

"PEOPLE WHO WERE NOTHING LIKE HIM, LIKED HIM"

If Joe Bloggs stopped his motorbike in the middle of the road and raised his hands to stop me and my vehicle, I am likely to think twice about stopping because he has no authority to act this way. But if that motorcyclist were a uniformed officer, they would immediately have my full attention. It is the same with preaching; some communicators represent no one else but themselves, whereas an ambassador of heaven on earth will carry a supernatural authority in what they say, compelling us to listen.

When commissioning those apprenticed by Him, Jesus *gave*

them power and authority.[18] As representatives of heaven on earth, we need to learn how to soar on the wings of the Holy Spirit and exercise God's *authority* – heaven's legal right to say what we are saying, to teach what we are teaching. Preaching is an event in which the Holy Spirit acts and speaks through frail, imperfect human beings. It is what the apostle Paul was describing when in 2 Corinthians 4:6–7 he talked about *the light of the knowledge of God's glory displayed in the face of Christ,* adding that *we have this treasure in jars of clay to show that this all-surpassing power is from God and not from us.* We are all jars of clay. Indeed, even the finest preachers are just cracked pots! It is through our human frailty that God's glory is made manifest.

GOD-GIVEN AUTHORITY ENABLES US TO DO WHAT WE ARE NOT NATURALLY ABLE TO DO

Overstepping the Mark

In terms of calling, we should avoid stepping outside our God-given sphere of influence. All Christ followers are called to "gossip the gospel", but not everyone is called to preach. Even those gifted to proclaim God's Word might

[18] Luke 9:1

discover that their gift is best exercised by bringing a homily to a small group. For others, it may be in a larger, more public setting. It is for the potential preacher and others to discover in which sphere their gifting best functions. It is dangerous prematurely to overstep our God-given boundaries. There is a place for, and a purpose in, our God-given limitation.

The apostle Paul recognised the importance of staying *within our sphere.*[19] He realised that there was a God-ordained boundary to his influence. As the ancient proverb states, *A man's gift makes room for him and brings him before the great.*[20] That said, our present boundaries could broaden. The word "sphere" comes from an ancient sporting background. It was used to mark the distance a javelin or discus thrower could reach. With exercise, practice, and training, the same thrower could increase their distance and range.

Timothy Keller reminds us that some Christians will have "one of these verbal gifts of counselling, instructing, teaching, evangelising", to which he adds "teaching

---

GODLY CONFINEMENT WILL EITHER BRING THE BEST OR THE WORST OUT OF US

---

19 2 Corinthians 10:12-18 esp. v.15, NASB

20 Proverbs 18:16, ESV

individuals and groups".[21] So, find the sweet spot of your God-given gifting and train to reach your full potential within your sphere. If you sense the call to preach and the only opportunity you presently have is to share with a small group, then be the best you possibly can be, and serve the purpose of God wholeheartedly.

TO STEP OUTSIDE YOUR PRESENT LINE OF DEMARCATION COULD DISQUALIFY YOU FROM BECOMING AN EFFECTIVE SERVANT OF THE KING

Missed Calls

Age does have some advantages. Over a lifetime spent in Christian circles, I have rejoiced in seeing so many *take the call* and fulfil their destiny in life. My own home church tithed its congregation in young men and women answering the call to minister God's Word. Sadly, however, I have also seen many who judged the cost to answer the call too high and chose rather to pursue a secular career.

Not everyone is called to devote their whole life to proclaiming God's Word, but if you are sensing a propelling force urging you into a full-time ministry to do something significant, then my appeal would be for you not to miss the call. I have observed people otherwise

[21] Timothy Keller, *Preaching: Communicating Faith in an Age of Scepticism.* See also Romans 12, Ephesians 4, and 1 Corinthians 12 and 14

engaged miss out on this incoming call. Then, having spent the best years of their lives doing something more lucrative, when facing retirement they try to reactivate a sense of calling, and all to no avail. Offering God our waning years, when we have wasted the best, seems insulting and undervaluing of this most glorious of opportunities. In a sacrificial act of full surrender, you will begin an adventure like no other.

IF GOD IS SPEAKING TO YOU ABOUT BECOMING A PREACHER, PICK UP THE CONNECTION NOW AND *TAKE THE CALL*

All this goes to show that what we understand as preaching – speaking about God's Word in a public setting – is not for everyone. We do not decide to be a preacher; we are called to preach. And although this heavenly compulsion might create a desire to run from such a calling, our insufficiency must learn to draw on God's all-sufficiency.

Maybe you have:

- A heavenly disturbance that has created a holy discontent
- The fruit of which is an inner compulsion to communicate truth
- And you are now struggling with a sense of personal inadequacy that

makes you want to run away from your calling

- Yet you have a deep hunger to minister, to do something significant with your life.

PREACHING IS NOT A PASTIME, A PART-TIME ACTIVITY WE SQUEEZE INTO OUR BUSY SCHEDULE

If this is you, I say, "Welcome to the call to preach!"

Preaching is not a pastime, a part-time activity we squeeze into our busy schedule; it requires a level of devotion that is not undertaken lightly. The call to preach will play havoc with your privacy and mess with your dreams and aspirations. It will become an all-consuming passion that overwhelms you. But if heaven is shaking your world, if you are reluctantly having to accept the reality that God is calling you to preach the Word,[22] I would strongly encourage you to listen, because if God is *making the call,* then drawing on Heaven's all-sufficiency, you should *take the call.*

22 Within a local church setting a call to preach is generally confirmed by others, particularly those mature leaders who sense and spot the call.

Discussion Points

- What, if anything, puts you off preaching in a public setting?

- Have you experienced a season of "holy disturbance" in your own life?

- How do you see yourself in terms of God's call on your life?

2 BE YOURSELF

The Holiday is a feel-good movie that tells the story of two women with guy problems. In an all-out effort to escape their dilemma, they decide to swap homes and exchange countries. For Iris (Kate Winslet), the turning point in a challenging long-term relationship comes during a conversation with an ageing Arthur Abbot (Eli Wallach). Playing the part of a famous screenwriter from the Golden Age of Hollywood, Abbot offers Iris some much-needed advice. Having explained that most movies have a leading lady and a best friend, Arthur says, "You, I can tell, are a leading lady, but for some reason, you're behaving like the best friend." Iris responds, "You're so right. You're supposed to be the leading lady of your own life." For Iris, this is a lightbulb moment.

Caught up in a copycat culture,

apprentice preachers can be obsessed with imitating their social media counterparts. Rather than taking the lead, they settle for the role of the understudy. Far from being a gender issue, the Leading Lady Syndrome is a personality crisis affecting many would-be preachers.

TOO MANY WOULD-BE PREACHERS ARE PLAYING THE ROLE OF THE "BEST FRIEND" INSTEAD OF THE "LEADING LADY"

Heaven is knocking on our dressing-room door telling us that we are needed on stage, but when fear turns a deaf ear, we run the risk of missing the call. God is shaking the shakeable to establish his unshakeable kingdom. We are living at a pivotal moment in time when a loving heavenly Father is calling people out to proclaim His Word. The issue is, will you *Take the Call,* and in doing so be sure to *Be Yourself*?

Critiquing 21st-century preaching as samey might sound harsh, but with so little by way of variety biblical preaching has become the property of the few. I don't want to lay the blame at the feet of a younger generation – who themselves are struggling to find their fit within today's church – because the fault lies elsewhere. Members of an older generation have not only failed to keep in step with an ever-changing culture; they have also dangled a leadership baton which they are reluctant to relinquish.

Too many local churches have become miniature manufacturing units. Taking in diverse, unique individuals, they use their old mechanisms to churn out standardised believers. When we fall into the mould of someone else's version of us, we rob the world of the wonders of God's grace. If the church continues to propagate this one-size-fits-all philosophy, diversity and creativity will go the way of the Dodo. Somewhere, somehow, would-be preachers are going to have to decide to be the best version of themselves they possibly can be.

THOSE SECURE IN THE BEST VERSION OF THEMSELVES GOD INTENDED, SHOULD NEVER FEEL THEY HAVE TO DISOWN, DISGUISE OR DEFEND IT

By its very nature, diversity will mean doing things differently. We must resist the pressures to make us into something God never intended. The real me "is what I think, judge, feel, value, honour, esteem, love, hate, fear, desire, hope for, believe in and am committed to".[1] So, do whatever it takes to stay true to the real you. When you are being true to the person God

[1] John Powell, *Why Am I Afraid to Tell You Who I Am?* (Fount, 1999)

intended you to be, you honour the work of the divine weaver who shaped you in your mother's womb. Yet, while the theory sounds wonderful, the practice can prove challenging. This charge to *Be Yourself* is met by internal and external forces conspiring to prevent people from becoming the best version of themselves they can be.

FEELINGS OF INADEQUACY SHOULD NOT BE ALLOWED TO SHAPE OUR IDENTITY OR OUR DESTINY

• INADEQUACY

Inadequacy is a common foe that we all confront, especially in the context of a call to preach. In his book *(Un)Qualified*, Steve Furtick writes, "I think we all secretly fight feelings of inadequacy, insufficiency and incompetence."[2] In his endorsement, Hillsong Church's senior pastor Brian Huston writes how this book "will resonate with each and every person who has ever felt the pull of calling and the inadequacy of their own humanity".

Maybe the apostle Paul was sensing this internal pressure when he wrote to the Corinthians: *I was with you in weakness and in fear and much trembling.*[3] In the same vein, he asked, *Who is sufficient for these*

2 Steve Furtick, *(Un)Qualified* (Multnomah Book, 2016)
3 1 Corinthians 2:3, ESV

things?[4] His glorious conclusion was, *God deliberately chose men and women that the culture overlooks . . . [He] chose these "nobodies" to expose the hollow pretensions of the "somebodies"? That makes it quite clear that none of you can get by with blowing your own horn before God.*[5]

The Bible is crowded with characters in whom the divine call triggered a negative response, born from low self-worth.

Jonah clearly didn't want the job and decided to run.

Moses made some feeble excuse about a speech impediment.

Gideon raised the issue of his lack of breeding.

Jeremiah brought up his immaturity.

Saul struggled with a level of insecurity that caused him to run and hide on the day of his coronation.

Some would argue that the apostle *Paul* spending three years in the Arabian desert was an attempt to run from his calling.

By playing host to feelings of inadequacy and unworthiness, we disqualify ourselves from experiencing God's sphere of

---

THE CALL TO PREACH WILL PLAY HAVOC WITH YOUR PRIVACY AND MESS WITH YOUR DREAMS AND ASPIRATIONS

---

[4] 2 Corinthians 2:16, ESV
[5] 1 Corinthians 1:26-31, MSG

excellence.

That said, feelings of insufficiency will do two things: they will stop us becoming self-reliant, self-opinionated, and self-promoting, and they will cause us to draw on God's all-sufficiency. Although the apostle Paul argued, *I stood before you feeling inadequate, filled with reverence for God, and trembling under the sense of the importance of my words,*[6] he also declared, *By the grace of God I am what I am, and his grace towards me was not in vain.*[7]

FEELINGS OF INADEQUACY AND UNWORTHINESS, ALTHOUGH NATURAL, ARE NOT NECESSARILY NEGATIVE

Learning to lean on God's supernatural ability, to do what we are not naturally able to do, needs to be a lesson learned in a Preaching 101 class. Naturally speaking, none of us measures up to the task, but by God's grace we negate the negative and become recipients of heaven's supernatural ability. Asking the question, *Who is adequate for these things?*[8] the apostle disarms this powerful foe by encouraging us to walk in the truth of 2 Corinthians 3:5-6: *our adequacy is from God, who also made us adequate as servants of a new covenant.*

God's opening gambit when introducing me to the role and

[6] 1 Corinthians 2:3, TPT
[7] 1 Corinthians 15:10, ESV
[8] 2 Corinthians 2:16, NASB

responsibility of preaching was to give me a life verse. Feeling inadequate and unworthy that God had *called [me] to preach on His behalf,*[9] I needed a biblical promise.

As with the other biblical heroes I just mentioned, Joshua must have felt somewhat overwhelmed. Having served a Moses generation, how could he match the faith and fortitude of those who had gone before? But then God spoke, *Moses my servant is dead. Now therefore arise, go over this Jordan . . . Every place that the sole of your foot will tread upon I have given to you . . . I will be with you. I will not leave you or forsake you. Be strong and courageous, for you shall cause this people to inherit the land.*[10]

WE FEEL INADEQUATE, BECAUSE NATURALLY-SPEAKING WE ARE

Whenever the occasion arises and the foe of inadequacy begins to rear its ugly head, I rehearse this promise. I know that if these forces are given a voice, they will seek to nullify God's call on my life. At the same time, the promise of heaven's presence gives me the courage to do what I am not naturally able to do.

- **INTIMIDATION**

There is a second force working

[9] Acts 9:15, paraphrased
[10] Joshua 1:1-6, ESV

with the first: intimidation. Whereas the first comes from within, this comes from people, objects, and events external to us.

Take the biblical account of the altercation between the prophet Elijah and the woman called Jezebel.[11] Her verbal threats so intimidated the preacher that he ran for his life. "Thank God, that doesn't happen today!" I hear you say. But the sad reality is, intimidation still occurs. When something or someone raises a threatening voice that gives you a burning desire to run and hide from the task of preaching, that is intimidation.

THERE IS PERHAPS NO FORCE MORE LIKELY TO SILENCE THE PROPHETIC PREACHER THAN THE VOICE OF INTIMIDATION

Like some overly zealous guard dog, threatening voices still make their presence known in the sphere of preachers and preaching. For example, there are intimidators who demand conformity to a certain type of preaching. Placing style over substance, old-school thinkers like these paint over the multi-coloured grace of God. Whether consciously or subconsciously, many of those in authority have a preferred style of preaching to which would-be preachers must conform. This of

11 1 Kings 19

course leads to bans on women being able to preach, especially where the pulpit has been the preserve of men alone. Sadly, I have seen how women have been barred from the exclusive, all-male, executive preaching suite. Believing that they are the last bastions of biblical tradition, some archaic and prejudicial leaders refuse to give access to those called to preach who look and sound different from them.

WHILE ONLY THOSE WHO TOE THE STYLISTIC PARTY-LINE ARE GIVEN THE OPPORTUNITY TO PREACH, DIVINE DIVERSITY BECOMES THE VICTIM

To those soft-spoken storytelling types, who represent a new and different voice and who stand in stark contrast to the norm of a loud, flashy, bombastic way of preaching, I would say, "Hang on! Your time is coming!" Old wineskins will break under the pressure of the new wine of a Holy-Spirit-driven renaissance. For the emerging generation who accept the importance of being themselves, I would say, "Do not listen to the voices of people trying to force on you a version of you that is clearly not authentic. A culture that forces others to fit into their traditional mould is, to say the least, childish; to say the worst, cultish."

To play the part of "the best friend" instead of "the leading lady", would be a sad indictment on a society crippled by intimidation. When a Davidic generation is forced to wear Saul's ill-fitting apparel and pretend to be what they are not, the world loses sight of the *many-coloured tapestry of God's grace.*[12]

IF OTHER PEOPLE HAVE A PROBLEM WITH YOU *BEING YOURSELF*, THEN THE PROBLEM IS WITH THEM, NOT YOU

If a good definition of preaching is *truth via personality*,[13] then the act of proclaiming God's Word is by its very nature a reflection of the preacher's emotions, decisions, and understanding. Every time we craft and preach a sermon, the Holy Spirit uses our unique individuality to bring glory to a loving heavenly Father.

Our personality is like the gilded picture frame that encompasses a masterpiece. The frame may look magnificent, but its role is to attract the attention of the onlooker so that they will gaze on the picture within its borders. When preaching becomes *truth via personality*, our words and actions might grab people's attention, but the ultimate purpose is to stop people in their tracks so that they gaze on the beauty of God in Christ.

12 1 Peter 4:10, TPT
13 Phillips Brooks (1835–1893) considered one of the great "princes of the pulpit", defined preaching as "the bringing of truth through Personality".

The Imitation Game

By allowing the forces of inadequacy and intimidation to define us, we participate in what, borrowing another movie phrase, I call "the imitation game". Most of us like to follow people who are further down the road from us. We watch their journey and check out their accomplishments. Now that well-known personalities have an online presence, we can track our preaching heroes 24/7. While this is a great opportunity to learn from others, the risk is that knowingly or unknowingly we begin to imitate those we appreciate.

OUR PERSONALITY, THOUGH USEFUL, SHOULD NOT DISTRACT FROM THE BEAUTY OF THE RISEN, GLORIFIED CHRIST

Although we admire the accomplishments of others, to mimic their methods and mannerisms not only devalues our unique contribution to civilisation but it ultimately destroys the diversity and creativity we bring to the table. Not everyone is a Beethoven or an Einstein, but there is beauty in the ordinary. Those who participate in the imitation game will never grow beyond their insecurity. They will become a mere facsimile of others.

When God created us, He knew exactly what He was doing. Although we may not have chosen the body or facial features we have, the reality is that the divine weaver has created in us a masterpiece of individuality. Those who become comfortable in their own skin should not *defend* or *disguise* the uniqueness of otherness.

A PHILOSOPHY OF ONE-SIZE-FITS-ALL HAS CREATED A CULTURE IN WHICH "THE BLAND ARE LEADING THE BLAND"

No One Likes a Fake!

I am a lover of the BBC television programme *Fake or Fortune.* Journalist Fiona Bruce teams up with art dealer Philip Mould to become "art detectives". In their investigations, they might travel from London to Paris, Amsterdam to South Africa, and from the banks of the Nile to New York to check the authenticity of a painting. Employing a team of experts, they use old-fashioned detective work and the latest forensic technology. The owners of each piece are taken on an emotional rollercoaster, while the viewer is held in a state of suspense. Expectation levels are raised when the experts suggest that this painting could be an unknown

Rembrandt, Picasso, Van Gogh, or Monet. Eventually the owners are faced with the reality of whether their painting is worth a fortune or, as they fear, is a fake of little monetary value.

The same truth plays out in the realm of preaching. Whatever type of preacher you are, determine to be the genuine article. In a world of copies, the church needs originals. Learn from those proficient as public speakers but determine to be the best version of yourself that you can possibly be.

YOU CAN ONLY RECOGNISE A COUNTERFEIT IF YOU ARE FAMILIAR WITH THE GENUINE

Tina and I used to watch our two young daughters play "church" on the front porch. Their cuteness was overwhelming. Using a hairbrush as a microphone, they took it in turns to place their hands on each other's head in an act of playful prayer. Their good-natured, good-humoured roleplay was captivating. Such childlike playful pretence, although far from reality, is something we saw a lot of in their early years. Imitation games are a normal feature of childhood. However, if this pretence continues into adulthood, the results may be tragic.

From Nike shoes to the daily news, fakes have become normalised. While it might be true that "no one likes a fake", the reality is that when the cost of the real becomes too expensive and our security is found in named brands, people prefer the fake.

PRETENDING TO BE WHAT WE ARE NOT MIGHT BE CUTE IN CHILDHOOD, BUT IN ADULTHOOD IT IS A CATASTROPHE

The Divine Weaver

You are unique. There never has been, nor will there ever be, another version of me or you. We are one-off people. Given the chance, we would probably like to change certain aspects of our physical appearance and modify certain past experiences – but the reality is, we are who we are. Sooner or later would-be preachers will have to accept that mind-boggling fact.

We are all wired differently. Difference is not wrong. It is just different. To be yourself is to pay your heavenly Father a compliment. Non-acceptance of this reality could potentially be viewed as accusing God of making a mistake. Praising the divine weaver for His work, the psalmist sings the following: *You formed my innermost being, shaping my delicate inside and my intricate outside, and wove them all together in my mother's womb.* He then adds, *I thank you, God, for making me so mysteriously complex! Everything you do is marvellously breath-taking. It simply amazes me to think about it! How thoroughly you know me, Lord!*[14]

So then, just in case you missed it, you are unique. There has never been or ever will be another you. Your disappointments, experiences, stories, understanding, emotions, success, and failings are all threads sown into the masterpiece that makes you, you. The mistakes in which you experienced God's redemptive grace can become part of the narrative through which you share the Good News. Read the biographical stories of those God uses and you discover how their mistakes became the material for God's ongoing redemptive story. Do not underestimate the power of your experience, people respond to authenticity; your life is a narrative that can be used to *Make the Mummies Dance.*

TO APPRECIATE AND ACCEPT OUR SIGNATURE SELF IS A MUST

[14] Psalm 139:13-14, TPT

Tell the Truth

Over the years, the American television show *Tell the Truth* has gone through a series of variations, both in the UK and USA. The basic idea of the show is that a panel of four celebrities is faced with three contestants who are challengers. Only one of these truly fits the brief of an unusual occupation or experience, which the host has already read to the celebrities. The panel then has a set time to ask each of the contestants some questions. Only the real person must tell the truth, whereas the impostors must tell convincing lies. When the panel has exhausted their questions and their time is up, the host will say, "Will the real ________ please stand up." After some bravado, the real contestant will rise to identify themselves.

GOD CAN USE WHAT YOU SO QUICKLY DISCARD

Life is not a game, and no matter how inadequate or intimidated we might feel, it is time to appreciate the masterpiece God has made us to be. Although the apostle Paul speaks of an ultimate revelation, there is a present reality to his words: *The entire universe is standing on tiptoe, yearning to see the unveiling of God's glorious sons and daughters!*[15] The host of heaven is shouting time on this generation, and the world is asking, "Will the real you please stand up!"[16]

INADEQUACY & INTIMIDATION ARE THE UGLY SISTERS THAT STOP US GOING TO THE BALL

15 Romans 8:19, TPT

16 As Chuck Swindoll says, "Know who you are," "Accept who you are," "Be who you are." "Preaching in the Prevailing Church, An Interview with Randy Pope", *Preaching*, 21, No. 4 (Jan–Feb 2006): 46.

Discussion Points

- Why do you think some people get caught up in a copycat culture?

- How do you see inadequacy and intimidation affecting your call to preach?

- What do you consider as the greatest challenge in *being the real you*?

3

FIND YOUR VOICE

Imagine for a moment you are an emperor penguin returning home from a month-long fishing trip. The challenge you now face is how to find your family among the hundreds of mirror images stretching out as far as the eye can see. In Antarctica, temperatures plummet to below minus 20 degrees centigrade. In a brave effort to avoid freezing to death, emperor penguins huddle in groups. Congregating in tightly packed communities, these flightless birds cleverly conserve heat and find shelter from the intense winds of the frozen tundra. Taking it in turns to stand on the outer edges of the group, these incredible creatures have learnt how to survive in sub-zero temperatures.

How does a penguin recognise their partner? With no nest or fixed point of reference, it would appear impossible. It's cold, noisy, and everyone looks the same. But these amazing birds have a secret weapon. Emperor penguins have a signature sound, a unique voice, that they use with great effect to find their mate. "Taking advantage of a quirk in the bird's anatomy, emperor penguins make a special two-voiced call which they use for individual recognition."[1] Such is the intricate magnificence of the natural world.

WE LIVE IN A NOISY ENVIRONMENT IN WHICH THERE ARE NUMEROUS VOICES CRYING OUT FOR OUR ATTENTION

The apostle Paul writes, *Does not nature itself teach you?*[2] Like the emperor penguin, we too have a signature sound that enables us to connect with other human beings. This unique sound is not a matter of diction, grammar, tone, accent, or punctuation – although they are important. This is about you finding your voice – being true to yourself and discovering the unique contribution you bring to the table of life. This will demand refusing to mimic others to become the best version of yourself you possibly can be.

There are, says the New Testament, *many kinds of voices in the world, and none of them is without signification.*[3] Differentiating between the

1 www.britannica.com/story/how-do-penguins-tell-each-other-apart
2 1 Corinthians 11:14, ESV
3 1 Corinthians 14:10, KJV

significant and insignificant is crucial for our long-term emotional and spiritual well-being. Just as every church needs to discover their own unique sound amidst the cacophony in their vicinity, would-be preachers need to appreciate their vocal DNA. They need the God-given ability to say things that no one else is saying, in a way that no one else is saying them. Heaven is calling out for a generation of preachers who will not only *take the call* and *be themselves* but *find their voice.* It is these secure individuals who will reconnect a lost generation to a loving heavenly Father. Knowing that someone, somewhere is waiting to hear your voice should spur you to discover your signature sound.

WITHOUT FINDING OUR VOICE WE WILL MERELY ADD TO THE NOISE OF AN ORPHANED GENERATION[4]

The Ketchup Conundrum

In the world of condiments taste is everything. Writing in *The New Yorker* magazine, Malcolm Gladwell introduces his readers to "The Ketchup Conundrum". His historical look at the food industry highlights how such things as mustard, spaghetti sauce, olive oil and salad dressing, to name a few, have over

[4] *'So often we continue to live as spiritual orphans, forgetting that thanks to the saving work of Jesus we have been made sons and daughters of God.' 'From Orphans to Heirs,'* Mark Stibbe, Bible Reading Fellowship, 2005

the years adapted into bestselling variations. While they all might have the same basic ingredients, it is how they are blended and balanced that has made the difference between success or failure. To help the reader understand this process, Gladwell likens food ingredients to musical notes. Although each note remains constant and true to itself, it is how the composer blends them that makes a one-off musical masterpiece. I might attempt to play Beethoven's *Moonlight Sonata* (1st Movement) and hit all the right notes in the right place, but take it from me, my rendition would be a poor substitute for hearing the same piece played by a trained concert pianist.

DIFFERENCE IS NOT WRONG IT IS JUST DIFFERENT

In the world of condiments, Heinz Ketchup is in a class of its own. Over the years, many have tried to equal or surpass what Henry John Heinz created, but since the late 1800s no one has been able to equal the unique blend and balance of his famous sauce – a sauce that year-on-year has continued to increase in popularity.[5]

Although all human voices have the same basic ingredients – pitch,

[5] Malcolm Gladwell, "The Ketchup Conundrum", *The New Yorker* (August 30, 2004).

tone, rhythm, tempo, and inflection – everyone is different. And while your voice might *sound* different from others, discovering your vocal DNA has more to do with *substance* than *sound*. Things we have *experienced,* the *emotions* we feel, what our *education* and *environment* have taught us, all these are the basic ingredients that help to create our individuality. Given time, the Holy Spirit will blend and balance these things in such a way as to produce a voice that says what no one else is saying, in a way no one else is saying it.

BY MARINATING IN THE PRESENCE OF THE HOLY SPIRIT, OUR VOICE WILL BECOME A BLEND AND BALANCE OF ALL THAT MAKES US UNIQUE.

Whenever my life has taken a major shift in direction, it has often been the result of a preacher or teacher who was saying something that no one else was saying and in a unique way. And before you ask, yes, like those in the early church, I did my due diligence by *examining the Scriptures daily to see if these things were so.*[6] Preachers and teachers like Henri Nouwen, Ern Baxter, John Poole, Arthur Wallis, Dr Martyn Lloyd-Jones, Dick Iverson, Jim Elliot, Kevin Conner, and Bryn Jones were all people whose unique voice enabled me to connect with a

[6] Acts 17:11, ESV

loving heavenly Father in a totally different way. Like them, we also get the privilege of bringing God's Word to life and in so doing *Make the Mummies Dance.*

It is fascinating that when God revealed Himself to the world in Christ, He described His son as *the Word.*[7] Jesus became for all humanity the visible and vocal representation of God's thoughts. As preachers, we are given the opportunity of voicing the mind of Christ to those willing to listen.[8] That heaven's life-giving power can be channelled through our speech is no small matter. As the biblical Proverb says, *Death and life are in the power of the tongue, and those who love it will eat its fruit.*[9]

NOTHING HAS MORE POTENTIAL FOR *MAKING THE MUMMIES DANCE* THAN A DIVINELY ANOINTED VOICE

When considering our vocal DNA, we should ask three key questions:

(1) Is your voice REALLY YOU?
Over a lifetime of preaching and teaching, I have admired many individuals, some of whom, in my early years, I sadly tried to imitate. Mimicking their style, turns of phrase, structure, and accent, the real me was hidden behind the disguise of trying to be what I

[7] John 1:1
[8] Matthew 11:15
[9] Proverbs 18:21, ESV

was not. At one time I thought an American accent added kudos. Then there was a time when I believed a Welsh inflection seemed to give me more spiritual gravitas. To roll the word *grace* off the tongue with a more guttural tone, seemed, at least in my warped mentality, to add a deeper spiritual significance to my preaching.

In this way, our listeners are not fixated on a façade or fooled by facsimiles. So, does what you say and the way you say it, truly reflect the real you? Often our insecurities and feelings of inadequacy will cause us to play games, to wear a mask, and become theatrical. This kind of behaviour will in the short-term adversely affect the depth, and in the long-term the parameters, of our spiritual communication with others.

WE WILL ONLY DISCOVER OUR VOCAL DNA WHEN WE SPEAK OUT OF THE AUTHENTIC SELF

From the most basic form of communication – sharing ideas, informing others of facts, and speaking in clichés – to the highest level of communicating gut level feelings, *finding our voice* is crucial. This journey of discovery will undoubtedly deepen our levels of confidence in who we are and what we say.

Like any communicator, preachers can play games. Our proclamations can become a cover-up when we put on a particular style to win over the audience. Preachers can take on such characters as *The Clown, The Cynic, The Conformist, The Dominator, The Bully, The Egghead, The Martyr* and the professional *Showman,* to name just a few.[10] When this happens, preaching becomes a performance that projects a false persona; it becomes a smokescreen for the real us. Everyone has their own God-given voice. The tragedy is that most people have yet to find it.

DOES YOUR VOICE REPRESENT THE REAL YOU OR ARE YOU FAKING IT?

We all tend to track famous individuals, becoming fascinated with their successes and with how they do things. And while the positive is that we can listen and learn from their activities, the negative side effect is that we can consciously or subconsciously begin to model what they say and how they say it.

(2) Is your voice OTHERWORLDLY?

The prophetic preacher presents the purposes of God to man.

[10] John Powell, *Why Am I Afraid to Tell You Who I Am?*

Inspirational in character and anointed in nature, these proclaimers of truth recognise where the listener is at and where in Christ they should be. As present-day *seers*, these *speakers* see through natural obstacles into the realm of God's supernatural opportunity. They speak of what the Holy Spirit has shown them.[11] With both feet firmly planted in the present, their words are otherworldly.

True biblical preaching needs to be both prophetic and *priestly*. Intercessory in nature, priestly preachers represent man's needs to God. They stand in the gap between earth and heaven. As go-betweens, they metaphorically take the hand of the listener and reconnect them to a loving heavenly Father. Bridging the gap between earth and heaven, they speak in such a way as to bring the prodigal home.

Clearly, Jesus had a voice that was otherworldly. In John 6, we find the disciples complaining about some teaching they found difficult to swallow. Explaining that his words were otherworldly,[12] Jesus offered them a get-out clause. While many took him up on the offer, the twelve

REPRESENTING THE INTERESTS OF GOD TO MAN, ALL PREACHING SHOULD BE *PROPHETIC* IN NATURE

[11] 1 Corinthians 2:10-16, NASB

[12] John 6:63, NASB, *the words that I have spoken to you are spirit, and are life*

concluded, *Lord to whom shall we go?* ***You have the words of eternal life.*** *We have come to believe and to know that you are the Holy One of God.*[13] How we need preachers today who speak words like these! Such anointed words interact with our spirit, causing our minds to line up with the truth, resulting in us walking in the good of what Jesus says.[14]

IF THERE WAS EVER A TIME WHEN THE CHURCH NEEDED PREACHERS TO STAND IN THE GAP, IT IS NOW

Following the Sermon on the Mount, Jesus' listeners *were astonished at his teaching, for he was teaching them as one* ***who had authority****, and not as their scribes.*[15] Completely secure in who He was and why He was present in that moment of time, Jesus spoke with authority. In this, His voice was different from the religious teachers of the day. It was truly *otherworldly!*

In a world deafened by so many voices, what is it that makes our words worth listening to? Preaching is an activity of the Holy Spirit and unless we learn to partner with Him, our disconnect from the purpose of heaven will continue. What will make our talk memorable and effective is people hearing the voice of God behind our voice.

Without the Holy Spirit, our

[13] John 6:68-69
[14] John 8:31,32
[15] Matthew 7:28-29, ESV

words will sound empty and lifeless. The same word used in Acts 2 to describe the ability *to **speak** with other tongues* is used in verse fourteen to describe Peter's capability to ***declare*** God's Word.[16] The same Holy Spirit who enables us to praise God supernaturally empowers us to preach God's Word prophetically.

In the process of discovering our signature sound, we will probably find that our voice will have a mixture of apostolic, prophetic, pastoral, teaching and evangelistic elements to it. While some preachers talk about the big picture, others will place us in the picture. Some will give us warm fuzzy feelings, while others will shake us to the core. Whether protecting or provoking us, the church needs the *governing* voice of the apostolic, the *guiding* voice of the prophetic, the *guarding* voice of the pastoral, the *grounding* voice of the teacher, and the *gathering* voice of the evangelist.

PEOPLE ARE WAITING TO HEAR WHAT YOU HAVE TO SAY AND HOW YOU SAY IT

(3) Is your voice LISTENED TO? The time between finding our voice and finding our audience is often long, lonely, and frustrating. If this is your story, *The Paul Potts*

16 See Acts 2:4,14 also 26:25 – the original word means *to speak out loudly and clearly, to speak with emphasis*

Phenomenon will prove encouraging.

At first glance, as a candidate for the television show *Britain's Got Talent,* Paul Potts did not look anything like a winner. A mobile phone salesman from South Wales, he dreamed of one day becoming an opera singer, something he believed he was born to become. Having listened to his dream, the judges made their disbelief audible. If Paul was to progress in the competition, he would have to change the judges' minds and win the hearts of the audience. Paul did not make his debut performance easy, either; he chose to sing the aria from the final act of Puccini's opera *Turandot*. It is called "Nessun Dorma".

LACKING SELF-CONFIDENCE, THIS DEMURE WELSHMAN HAD FOUND HIS VOICE, HE WAS NOW ABOUT TO DISCOVER HIS AUDIENCE

From the very first sound, his raw talent wowed both the judges and the audience. Having struggled for years, Paul Potts had already found his voice. Now, however, his unique voice had discovered its audience.

Just as the English football star Marcus Rashford (food poverty) and the Swedish activist Greta Thunberg (climate change) have found their voice both nationally and internationally, so the would-be preacher needs to find their voice. In the meantime, we should not become overly concerned with finding an audience. First find your voice and the audience will follow. When the Holy Spirit begins to blend and balance our vocal DNA, causing us to say what no one else is saying, in a way that no one else is saying it, an audience will automatically gather. When your words become a refreshing change from the bland and the boring, your voice will give you a place at the table.

FOR THE BODY OF CHRIST TO REACH ITS FULL STATURE, IT NEEDS TO EXPERIENCE THOSE VOICES THAT ARE OTHERWORLDLY IN NATURE

When Jesus stepped into a morbid environment to raise Lazarus from the dead, He literally made a mummy dance.[17] The disappointment, caused by His seeming delay, did little if anything to deflect Jesus from His purpose. Speaking life to the mourners and liberty to the mummified remains of Lazarus, Jesus literally *Made the Mummies Dance.* Secure in the knowledge of who He was, Jesus spoke life-giving words that caused His listeners to say, *"No one ever spoke like this man!"*[18]

Within an intimate relationship with a loving heavenly Father, we will receive revelatory truth. Once

[17] John 11:1-44
[18] John 7:46, ESV

we start preaching out of this rich treasure trove of truth, our words will cause listeners to buy into and build on what they hear. So, the question needs to be this: are we acting as originals, or continuing to behave like copies?

God's Renaissance Man

FUNDAMENTAL TO FINDING OUR VOICE IS A GROWING AWARENESS OF WHO WE ARE IN CHRIST

We cannot allow our insecurities to shape our voice. Fearful of saying what no one else is saying, we capitulate to commonly held views. Surrendering to the status quo will cause us to become an *echo* rather than a *voice*.

John the Baptist was God's Renaissance Man. Standing on the edge of history between the Old and New Testaments, John ushered in a whole new administration as ***the voice** of one crying out in the wilderness.*[19] To say that John the Baptist was unique is an understatement. His diet, dress, desert dwelling, and general demeanour were lightyears away from the world into which he spoke. John's manner was so diverse that when the disciples returned from observing him, Jesus remarked,

[19] John 1:23, ESV

"He was not what you thought, was he?"[20] When was the last time you heard a congregation say that about last Sunday's preacher? Even so, although John was a class act, he was only the warm-up for the main event yet to come.

Today, God is raising up a John-the-Baptist generation, Christ followers who live a lifestyle of total dependence on God. Opposing all things religious, they are deeply relational proclaimers of God's Word. These revelatory preachers will say things no one else is saying. Living a life of holy separation, their utterances will have a cutting edge to them, *Laying an axe to the root of the trees.*[21] Uprooting the religious spirit, their unique voice will bring *times of refreshing from the presence of the Lord.* Refusing to be an *echo* – repeating what others are already saying – this John-the-Baptist generation will be a *voice* declaring revelatory truth that is spoken with divine authority.[22]

To continually state the obvious will be insufficient. Preaching is an activity of the Holy Spirit and as such preachers need to partner with the executor of God's will. Being

FINDING YOUR VOICE, GIVES YOU *A VOICE!*

[20] Matthew 11:2-19, paraphrased
[21] Matthew 3:10
[22] 1 Corinthians 11:23; Galatians 1:12; Isaiah 33:18; Revelation 2:17; Proverbs 2:1

otherworldly, Spirit-filled preachers will experience an interaction of the Holy Spirit with their spirit, causing them to say the right thing, at the right time, in the right way. This will be effective and productive because what first grips you will ultimately grip others.

SEEING BEYOND OUR IMMEDIATE INTO THE REALM OF GOD'S ULTIMATE IS THE ESSENCE OF WHAT IT MEANS TO BE A PROPHETIC PREACHER

Hear the Call

What if God is *making the call* to a generation of would-be preachers, those people secure enough to *be themselves* and work hard at *finding their voice* – a John-the-Baptist generation willing to pay the price of solitude and separation? What if God is calling preachers who are not looking to win a popularity competition, but openly and honestly declare God's absolute truth? Moving in fresh revelation, such preachers will usher in a wave of resurrection life in our towns and cities. They will be seen *Making the Mummies Dance.*

Rather than hearing echoes of some bygone era – old-school preachers stuck in a time warp – the world needs to hear men and women who have found their signature sound and who have begun to vocalise God's truth in a way that points people to a better future. During this pandemic, I have seen self-isolating Italians taking to their balconies to form an impromptu communal choir. They have found their voices. Meanwhile reserved English people would every Thursday at 8pm stand on their doorstep to applaud and cheer the heroic efforts of the health service. They have found their voice too. Now it's time for the voice of the church to be heard as well!

In God's economy, it is midnight. Like Paul and Silas in lockdown,[23] it's time to sing from our place of confinement. It's time for would-be preachers to break out of their self-imposed incarceration and declare the goodness of God to those within their present sphere of influence. For too long, a Cinderella culture has paralysed the church, allowing the ugly sisters of inadequacy and intimidation to exile would-be preachers. We have allowed others to taunt us and stop us living in our calling.

It's time to break free from basement thinking about ourselves

IF THE GLOBAL PANDEMIC OF 2020 HAS TAUGHT US ANYTHING IT IS THAT THE CHURCH NEEDS TO REDISCOVER ITS PROPHETIC VOICE

[23] Acts 16:16-40

and start enjoying the high-level living of God's call on our lives.

It's time to escape the ghetto mentality and step onto our balconies and proclaim the message of God's grace.

It's time to applaud the goodness of God in our lives in a way that causes the Good News to reverberate around our neighbourhoods.

IT'S TIME FOR WOULD-BE PREACHERS TO *TAKE THE CALL, BE THEMSELVES* AND *FIND THEIR VOICE*

It's time for the earth to hear heaven's anthem with lyrics that speak of a loving heavenly Father waiting with open arms to receive His prodigal sons and daughters.

It's time!

Discussion Points

- Are you a Heinz Ketchup person, or a cheap, supermarket imitation?

- How do you see God using the ingredients of your past to create your vocal DNA?

- How do the Paul Potts, Marcus Rashford, or Greta Thunberg stories speak to you?

4 CREATE A PEARL

No matter what you think of his personality, Steve Jobs was the consummate communicator. He could take a piece of boring technology and make it live. Possessing evangelistic fervour, he could grab people's attention from the word go. Answering questions that everyone was asking, his presentations were transformative. When Steve Jobs talked, the world listened. In an atmosphere full of expectation, people bought into whatever Jobs was selling. His listeners were left in no doubt that this was an item essential for everyday life, and that without it, no one could truly function.

In his book, *The Presentation Secrets of Steve Jobs,* Carmine Gallo writes, "Whether he's introducing the new iPhone or delivering a keynote presentation, Steve Jobs electrifies audiences with his incomparable style and showmanship. He doesn't just convey information in his presentations; he tells a story, paints a picture, and shares a vision."[1] As a storyteller, artist, and visionary, Steve Jobs illustrated the level of investment needed to become a great communicator. If this man teaches us anything about public speaking, it is that *great presentations require extensive preparation.*

ALTHOUGH YOUR LISTENER MAY NOT PHYSICALLY WALK OUT, THEY CAN CHECK OUT MENTALLY

Having a misguided sense of security some preachers have concluded that their congregation is too polite to walk out on their talks. While members of the public would think nothing of leaving a movie, preachers assume that church attendees would never exit a place of worship in the same way. Taking people for granted like this is unwise. With the internet at their fingertips, people are easily disengaged. What you might naively believe is electronic notetaking or Bible reading may well be a bored listener checking emails or playing a computer game. Non-engaging sermons lead to non-engaged listeners – people who may be present in body but

1 Carmine Gallo, *The Presentation Secrets of Steve Jobs* (McGraw Hill, 2010)

absent in mind and spirit.

It's All in The Preparation

Some sixty years on, I can still hear the words of my old music teacher ringing in my ears. "Christopher," she would say (whether it was my mother or my music tutor, using my full name was never a good sign!). "Christopher, you need to practise, practise, practise." Waving the carrot of a possible music degree in my face, Mrs Smith tried her best to coerce a disinterested eleven-year-old to become a disciplined musician who practised the piano for one hour each day, five days a week. She hoped that affirming my latent talent would change my lazy behaviour. However, what I had neglected became abundantly clear to her finely tuned musical ear. My weekly lessons became a pitiful performance, rarely improved by cramming. That I only ever attained Grade One Music Theory says more about my lack of preparation than it does about the persistence of a very patient tutor. Preparing to preach takes a serious investment of time. Creating a transformative

A PREACHER'S POOR PERFORMANCE IS OFTEN ROOTED IN A LACK OF PERSONAL PREPARATION

experience in your listeners requires a great deal of practice. Although there is no set formula for the time required, some have suggested that a thirty-minute talk can take up to fifty hours of thinking, reading, researching, sketching, praying, and writing time. A little excessive you might think, but Nancy Duarte, the mastermind who turned Al Gore's 35mm slides into an award-winning documentary *(An Inconvenient Truth)* suggests that "a presenter [should] spend up to ninety hours to create an hour-long presentation that contains thirty slides".[2] Even when taking out the six hours she allocates for slide preparation, you still have a major investment of time. Other secular speechwriters use a simple equation: a thirty-minute talk will take the same number of hours in preparation.

IF OUR PREACHING IS TO COMMUNICATE CHANGE RATHER THAN TRANSFER INFORMATION, PREPARATION IS VITAL

Would-be preachers need to wake up to the reality that it takes time to prepare a transformative sermon. Preachers who shortcut the preparation process do little to honour the preaching gift or help the listener to find the breakthrough in their lives. As one of the greatest twentieth-century preachers said, "If

[2] Carmine Gallo, *The Presentation Secrets of Steve Jobs*

you are one of those who find you take less than 4-5 hours to prepare a message, I can only be thankful to God I don't have to sit and listen to it!"[3] That may sound a bit harsh, but the truth is this: thorough sermon preparation is the basic groundwork on which everything else is built. Though invisible to others, the work will pay dividends.

LIKE ANY PIECE OF CIVIL ENGINEERING, GROUNDWORK IS TIME-CONSUMING, COSTLY, AND OFTEN MESSY, BUT NEVERTHELESS ESSENTIAL

Begin at the Beginning

So, you've been asked to preach. But right now, you're staring at a blank page or an empty screen. The deadline looms and you have no idea what you're going to share. You need a creative spark, something that fires the spirit and illuminates the mind.

Preachers are passionate people, driven by a divine purpose. They experience what the prophet Jeremiah describes as *fire shut up in [his] bones.*[4] It is this flash of inspiration, a *eureka* moment, that sets the creative process in motion. Whether it's a song, story or sermon we all need that embryonic thought that, given time, will develop into a fully formed piece of work.

[3] Bryn Jones, *Homiletics,* 1985 Seminar
[4] Jeremiah 20:9, ESV

The trouble is you never know how or when a creative idea will strike. All verbal and non-verbal communication begins with a unique thought. Whether it is a good or godly idea will take time, experience and mentoring to determine.

WHETHER IT IS A STORYLINE, SONG LYRIC OR SERMON, EVERY NARRATIVE BEGINS WITH A CREATIVE IDEA

Authors, songwriters, poets, and preachers all look for that lightbulb moment, that flash of inspiration that kickstarts the creative process. But often those ideas rarely work in tune with our lifestyle. We therefore need to be constantly prepared to capture a *Spark,* cultivate a *Seed* and give that grain of *Sand* time to develop to its full potential.

(1) SPARKS that light a Fire

The Autumn of 1666 was the dawn of a perfect storm: ten months of drought, the remnants of the Great Plague, houses built of timber and straw; people living close together. Here was a tinder-box situation in which one careless spark was to ignite an inferno. The Great Fire of London destroyed 13,000 houses, 87 churches and caused thousands of deaths. In the end, it was discovered that this occurred because the housemaid to Thomas

Farynor, residing in Pudding Lane, failed to douse a fire in the bakery oven.

Who knows what long-term effects a flash of inspiration may have on your town or city when it first smoulders in you before igniting others? The spark of an idea is often short-lived, transient, easily lost. As the Scriptures say *sparks fly upwards*[5] and disappear. If that lightbulb moment is to realise its full potential we need to capture the spark. As a woodsman produces a spark to light a fire, he will quickly surround it with combustible material. Just as a petrol engine needs fuel to convert an electrical ignition into movement, so those ideas, no matter how random, need to be contained. For that to happen we need to be prepared for the unexpected. "Be alert for writing ideas you find unexpectedly as you shop, drive, goof around, or walk home from school. Watch for unusual events, persons, objects, or conversations. For example, you might come across an obviously well-cared-for, healthy plant perched on the porch of a neglected, ramshackle home. A 'flower-in-the-rough' scene such

A SINGLE SPARK IS SUFFICIENT TO SET A WHOLE CITY ALIGHT

[5] Job 5:7, MSG

as this one could bring to mind a number of writing subjects."[6]

Sir Arthur Conan Doyle's fictional character Sherlock Holmes was a masterful detective. He was forever filling scrapbooks with odd bits of information, news articles, stories, quotes, observations, and thoughts that would eventually enable him to crack the case he was working on. Whether using a keyboard or a pen, we need to create a process of recording our thoughts, ideas, and themes, no matter how random.

WOULD-BE PREACHERS NEED TO BE READY TO RECORD THE SPARK OF AN IDEA BEFORE IT VANISHES

Working sixty-hour weeks in shopfitting and trying to pioneer a church at the same time, I would often have the spark of an idea at the most inconvenient moment. It was not unusual to return home with ideas for a sermon scribbled on a piece of scrap timber. What seemingly was an insignificant, random thought needed to be captured before it faded. That burning idea that comes while walking the dog or driving to and from work, may be sufficient to start you on a journey that culminates in a transformative sermon. No matter how seemingly irrelevant or deconstructed our thoughts may be,

6 Write Source, Writers INC (Educational Publishing House, 1992)

we need to foster a habit of storage,[7] because that flash of inspiration might light a fire that eventually ignites a whole city.

So, I hoard creative thoughts the same way I save pieces of timber, thinking that one day I will create something beautiful from that length of wood. It may end up as firewood, but burning timber still at least keeps people warm!

(2) SEEDS that produce a Harvest

Always be prepared to capture a spark and cultivate a seed of truth. *Let our gardener, God, landscape you with the Word, making a salvation-garden of your life.*[8] If our minds are open and our hearts ready, our Gardener-God will sow an abundance of seed in us. Just remember, though, if the *seed is crowded out [by] worrying about tomorrow, making money, and having fun,*[9] then it is likely to be lost. By removing personal obstacles and resisting the enemy's distractions, we prepare ourselves for the Holy Spirit to propagate the seed truths our Gardener-God has sown. Creating the spiritual "greenhouse effect" of a right environment for the seeds, we clear our minds of

EVERYONE HAS THE CAPACITY TO RECEIVE A CREATIVE IDEA.

[7] Some people use SIRI, iPhone Voice Notes, Google Assistant to record their ideas.
[8] James 1:21, MSG
[9] Luke 8:14, MSG

the temporal to meditate on the eternal. By reading widely, listening carefully, and observing intently, we prepare our minds to propagate what God has given. All heavenly seed carries within it the potential to reproduce after its own kind, but it needs the right environment to germinate and grow.

GIVEN THE RIGHT ENVIRONMENT, SEEDS OF TRUTH WILL GERMINATE AND GROW

Some would-be preachers are *surface or shallow thinkers,* undisciplined in their thought processes. They may initially show great enthusiasm, but then they lack the commitment necessary to develop an idea, becoming easily distracted by temporal things. Then there are the *cluttered thinkers* who half-heartedly receive an idea, only to allow external pressures to ruin what is potentially a life-changing seed truth.

We can all be recipients of divine seeds, whatever our age, educational background, or level of spiritual maturity. If the best preachers are yet to come, they will emerge from a generation of "uncluttered thinkers",[10] men and women willing to spend quality time to both capture the spark and cultivate the seed. Such people will be committed to nurturing the kind

[10] Luke 10:21, NASB, *"infants"* meaning those with unsophisticated, uncluttered minds.

of revelation that will teem in their minds and hearts before ever they think of packaging and distributing it to others in an accessible and nourishing form.

Never forget that being given the opportunity to teach or preach God's Word in any setting is a privilege.

THE OPPORTUNITY TO PARTNER WITH THE HOLY SPIRIT AND DELIVER HEAVEN'S WILL ON EARTH IS SOMETHING THAT SHOULD NEVER BE UNDERESTIMATED

(3) SAND that creates a Pearl

Many of my ideas for a book, blog, sermon, or article begin with a *holy irritant,* a thought that sticks in my mind no matter how hard I try to shake it off. This can go one of two ways. I can either react negatively or respond positively. While the former tends to be destructive, the latter, with God's help, is constructive. Let me give you an example. The writing of *Making the Mummies Dance* began with a *holy irritant.* Tired of listening to snore-inducing sermons and preachers mimicking TED-type Talks (whose only redeeming factor was their brevity), I decided to commit pen to paper. This was a holy irritant that will hopefully, and by God's grace, produce a pearl or two of wisdom for others to enjoy.

Dr Martin Luther King Jr. said, "I

cannot stand idly by and not raise my voice against something that I see as wrong. Now there are those who say . . . 'What are you doing speaking out?' . . . I am a preacher of the gospel. And when my father and others put their hands on my head and ordained me to the Christian ministry, it was a commission. And something said to me that the fire of truth is shut up in my bones, and when it burns me, I must tell it."[11] Here is a prophetic and priestly preacher inspired to speak out because of holy discontent.

WHETHER YOUR AUDIENCE IS TWELVE OR TWELVE HUNDRED, YOUR LEVEL OF PREPARATION REMAINS THE SAME

When a grain of sand gets into an oyster it causes the creature to secrete a shell-like substance (nacre) to coat the intruder, which over time produces a high-valued pearl. A verbal jewel such as preaching may well begin with a holy irritant. Instead of dismissing it as something oppressive, we need to allow time for God's grace to do its work. What began as an irritation can become a priceless pearl of wisdom, something which the listener will go to great lengths to make their own and apply in their daily lives. Learning the art of preparation will mean we capture a creative *Spark,* cultivate the *Seed* of

11 Minister and Civil Rights Activist, Dr Martin Luther King, Jr.

truth, and allow time for that speck of *Sand* to produce a pearl of great wisdom. As we read in Matthew 13, when people find treasure in a field or a pearl of great price, they *sell all that they have*[12] to obtain it.

Create a Pearl

In our preparation, we need to keep the endgame in view. Our ultimate desire is that the listener will buy into the truth we are sharing. More than anything, we want them to come to a place where they are ready to pay the price to secure God's rule in their lives. When this happens, an eternal transaction takes place. If we prepare well, the Holy Spirit will present our listeners with a priceless pearl, a truth which they are willing to sacrifice everything to buy.

WHAT BEGAN AS A HOLY IRRITATION CAN BECOME A PRICELESS PEARL OF WISDOM

The downcast have been uplifted, the tired have found hope, the battle-weary have been inspired to fight on, and the discouraged have found courage. Think of Winston Churchill's, "We will fight them on the beaches", John F. Kennedy's inaugural address, "My fellow Americans, ask not what your country can do for you. Ask

12 See Matthew 13:44

what you can do for your country", William Wilberforce's speeches about the abolition of the slave trade before the House of Commons, or Franklin Delano Roosevelt's words, "December 7, 1941 – a date which will live in infamy." There are so many examples. Abraham Lincoln's Gettysburg Address, "Four score and seven years ago our fathers brought forth on this continent, a new nation." Martin Luther King Jr., "I have a dream." Jesus Christ's Sermon on the Mount. All these began with a flash of inspiration, a seed thought, and in many cases, a holy irritant.

THROUGHOUT HISTORY, GREAT ORATORS HAVE USED THE POWER OF WORDS TO CHANGE LIVES

Good preparation is the key. A concert pianist will always advocate the importance of practice, while in the same breath admitting that they never do as much as they should. Why is that? Human nature is always looking for the easy option, the shortcut that alleviates the cost involved in preparation. The insatiable appetite for instant gratification demands the destination without the journey. Yet God Himself prepares. The Bible says of the Christ follower, *Even before we were born, God planned* ***[prepared]*** *in advance our destiny and the good works we would do to fulfil it.*[13] When Jesus came into the world, *He said, "Sacrifices and offerings you have not desired, but a body have you **prepared** for me."*[14] Even now the ascended Christ has gone *to **prepare** a place for you.*[15] God is not haphazard. He is never winging it or jumping onto lastminute.com. He prepares and so should we in the task of preaching. Great presentations require intensive preparation.

WHILE THE POWER OF WORDS IN GENERAL IS IMMENSE, THE IMPACT OF *ANOINTED* WORDS IS IMMEASURABLE

---

[13] Ephesians 2:10, TPT
[14] Hebrews 10:5, ESV
[15] John 14:3, TPT

Discussion Points

- What can you learn from Steve Jobs' communication skills?

- What, in your opinion, is the point of practising a sermon?

- How do you capture the spark of an idea?

5 MOVE BEYOND THE MARGINS

I'm a lover of movies and this passion recently morphed in an autobiographical book called *The Reel Story*. Rooted in my ten favourite movies, I share the lessons learned and mistakes made in a lifetime spanning three-quarters of a century. The one cinematic classic that failed to make the final cut was *Patch Adams*. The true story of Hunter "Patch" Adams, this American biographical comedy-drama (starring the inimitable Robin Williams) is a must-see movie. Playing the part of a misunderstood doctor who wants to use humour and pathos to treat his patients, Williams finds himself clashing with the medical profession and confronting his own sense of failure. Struggling with suicidal thoughts, he voluntarily admits himself into a mental institution. By helping his fellow inmates, Patch

Adams finds a fresh purpose in life.

Among the many wonderful moments in the movie there is one scene inside the hospital that perfectly illustrates the essence of what it means to *Move Beyond the Margins.* While wandering around the institution, Adams meets a fellow inmate called Arthur Mendelson (Harold Gould). A wealthy mathematician, it is Mendelson who first gives Patch his nickname. It is through this meeting of minds that Adams gains a fresh perspective on life.

PARTNERING WITH THE HOLY SPIRIT, OUR SERMON PREPARATION NEEDS TO BECOME A VISIONARY EXPERIENCE

Entering Mendelson's room, Patch is desperate to find the answer to a simple equation Mendelson has posed. Holding up four fingers, Mendelson asks Patch how many he can see. When Patch says "four" Mendelson reprimands him. "If you focus on the problem you can't see the solution," Mendelson says. "Never focus on the problem . . . Look beyond the fingers . . . See what no one else sees. See what everyone else chooses not to see out of a fear of conformity and laziness. See the whole world anew each day." Looking beyond the immediate, Patch begins to see the ultimate. He sees the blurry form of eight fingers.

Seeing the Unseen

All preaching needs to be prophetic. As God's prophetic mouthpieces, proclaimers of His Word need to see what no one else sees so that they can say what no one else is saying. Partnering with the Holy Spirit, our sermon preparation needs to become a visionary experience. Stating the obvious is no longer sufficient. Educating the mind will not, on its own, initiate the spiritual transformation humanity so desperately needs. Fundamental to all prophetic proclamation is our willingness to co-labour with the Holy Spirit so that we can see beyond the surface of things and gain a heavenly perspective on the biblical text.

TRANSFORMATIONAL SERMONS LOOK BEYOND MAN'S IMMEDIATE INTO GOD'S ULTIMATE

My wife Tina loves puzzles. Whether it is a word puzzle, number puzzle, picture puzzle, or jigsaw puzzle, she loves the journey as much as the destination. Knowing this, I recently gave her the gift of a *Wasgij*. What on earth is that? I hear you say. The clue is in the word. *Wasgij* is *Jigsaw* spelt backwards. What normally would take Tina hours to complete, took days. Although the picture on the box resembles the puzzle inside, it is taken from a different geographical or historic perspective. As such, it offers little help. To complete the puzzle, you must literally think outside the box. Like Patch Adams seeing beyond the four fingers, or Tina constructing a Wasgij – a puzzle formed out of a familiar image from an unfamiliar angle and time frame – would-be preachers have to sharpen their perceptive skills in order to move beyond the margins.

PROPHETIC PROCLAIMERS ARE TOTALLY OVERWHELMED WITH THE PURPOSES OF GOD

Prophetic proclaimers are totally overwhelmed with the purposes of God. Their prayer is that *the eyes of [people's] understanding will be flooded with light, so that they may know the inheritance they have in Christ Jesus.*[1] Prophetic preachers take people out of the valleys to the mountaintops to show them what Christ has made possible. Inspired by this godly perspective, they move beyond the margins that people, objects, and events might have imposed on them, transitioning both themselves and others into all that is theirs through

[1] Ephesians 1:18, paraphrased

the redemptive work of Christ.

For preachers to create this level of transformative breakthrough, they must first approach the Scriptures *microscopically and telescopically.*

(1) Microscopic – Looking into the Detail

Having captured the spark of an idea, the would-be preacher now steps into a season of personal preparation. Whether you are taking a *topical, expositional,* or *textual*[2] approach to a Bible passage, the preparatory process will require detailed investigation. Giving serious consideration to the text involves thinking, reading, meditating, researching, writing, and sketching out your rough ideas. This joyous yet sometimes arduous journey will, if taken seriously, culminate in a singular theme, a message that has clarity, beauty, imagination, humour, and passion. "That one message, idea, principle, or truth that [has] to be delivered at all cost. The one thing isn't just information. It is not just a carefully crafted phrase. It is literally a burden that weighs so heavily on the heart of the communicator that he or she must deliver it."[3]

"FIND THAT ONE MESSAGE, IDEA, PRINCIPLE OR TRUTH THAT HAS TO BE DELIVERED AT ALL COST"

2 *Topical* preaching involves speaking on themes that are related to life, for example family life, marriage, leadership. *Expositional* preaching is a systematic explanation of the Bible. *Textual* preaching is when we analyse a particular verse or passage of Scripture within its context alone and without placing it within a broader setting.

3 Andy Stanley and Lane Jones, *Communicating for a Change,* p. 113

Looking for clues as to what God is saying, the potential speaker turns detective and scientist. Carrying out a biblical autopsy on the text, they cut with forensic precision deep into the inner workings of God's Word. Opening the outer margins of the text, the speaker-turned-student will read and re-read the relevant verses. Cross-referencing the text, he or she begins to gain an insight into the historic, cultural, geographic, and linguistic make-up of a particular portion of Scripture. More than simply scanning the surface, the student's quest is to discover the true meaning the Holy Spirit intended when first inspiring the writer. All the while, the student is asking such questions of the text: What does it say? What does it mean? What does it say to us today?

WITH FORENSIC PRECISION CARRY OUT A BIBLICAL AUTOPSY ON THE TEXT

Without becoming overly forensic, we need to correctly dissect the Scriptures and to study the text within its context. Using various study tools, the student learns how to bridge the linguistic, cultural, geographic, and historical gaps that exist between the original text and 21st-century Christian living. This is not a mere casual glance at the text, a skimming over the scriptural surface. This is the moment in which transformational preachers begin to gain a heavenly insight into the inspired text. "To interpret and apply the biblical text in accordance with its real meaning, is one of the preachers most sacred duties."[4]

While the tyranny of the urgent might try to hijack all this, a season of prayerful solitude and thoughtfulness will enable the would-be preacher to marinate in the textual truth of God's Word.[5] Through biblical meditation, we *let the word of Christ dwell in [us] richly*[6] and become *a workman who has no cause to be ashamed, correctly analysing and accurately dividing [rightly handling and skilfully teaching] the Word of Truth.*[7]

DON'T LET THE URGENT HIJACK THE IMPORTANT

Even if we are not naturally detailed people, preachers cannot afford to either skip or shortcut this crucial part of the preparatory process. *Der liebe Gott steckt im detail* is an ancient German proverb which translated means, "God is in the detail." Be interested in every detail, even if all your discoveries do not make it into the final cut of

[4] Based on a quote by John A. Broadus, *On the Preparation and Delivery of Sermons* (Titus Books, 2014)
[5] 1 Timothy 4:14-16
[6] Colossians 3:16, ESV
[7] 2 Timothy 2:15, AMP

your sermon.

However, there needs to be balance between the microscopic and the macroscopic. Too much detail, while fascinating for the researcher, might be too much for the listener. Then again, the lack of detailed investigation might prompt the speaker to cement over the ill-prepared cracks that appear in their sermon. Using sermon fillers like irrelevant stories, jokes, and theological rabbit holes only confirms a preacher's lack of preparation.

PREACHERS OF GOD'S WORD MUST FIRST AND FOREMOST BECOME SCHOLARS OF HIS WORD

The craft of sermon preparation gives us a clear insight into the artistry needed to create a transformative message. Taking the basic biblical material, the preacher begins to form their argument. With a visual picture in their minds of what the finished article will look like, they remove and replace words, phrases, and biblical references as a sculptor does when working with a lump of clay. Creating a message that will ultimately bring glory to God, they diligently fashion their words into what they visualised in their minds.

(2) Telescopic – Looking into the Distance

DeVern Fromke described this process perfectly when he wrote, "In each generation, God always has had those men [and women] whose framework of vision reached beyond the general consciousness to see God's larger purpose. They lived and breathed with a divine destiny consciousness imparted by God. Such [people] always moved beyond the narrow vision of their day."[8] That is "telescoping". Seeing God's big picture, in a way that causes us to live and breathe our immediate in the light of His ultimate, is true kingdom living.

LIVE YOUR IMMEDIATE IN THE LIGHT OF THE ULTIMATE

Often students of the Word fail in doing due diligence to the text because they are fearful of moving beyond the well-defined margins set by others. Constrained by their education, environment, or experience, they fail to move beyond those well-defined margins into God's bigger picture. The mind of man can become a sieve that weakens the Word by reducing a powerful revelation down to the common denominator of what we

[8] DeVern Fromke, *Unto Full Stature* (Sure Foundation Publishers, 1985)

have previously heard or experienced. Yes, read what others have to say, but remember prophetic preaching is an out-of-the-box thinking process that will result in you saying what no one else is saying, in a way that no one is saying it. To be sure that your ideas are biblically sound, find yourself a spiritual sponsor, a critical friend, someone who will both challenge and champion your call to preach.

THE THINKING OF PREVIOUS GENERATIONS CAN TURN GROOVES INTO GRAVES IN WHICH ORIGINALITY IS BURIED

There is said to be a roadside sign in Alaska that reads, "Choose your rut carefully, you'll be in it for the next two hundred miles." The grooves in the ground were created by different people travelling in the same way as others before them. As in the natural so in the spiritual. Well-worn denominational grooves can so easily become the graves in which subsequent travellers become stuck.

Ask the Holy Spirit to help you move beyond the manmade traditions of previous generations. Just as Patch Adams saw beyond the obvious, so the Holy Spirit can take us beyond the printed page into the heart of a loving heavenly Father. As the apostle Paul reminds the

Corinthians, *For to us God revealed them* – the things eye has not seen, and ear has not heard – *through the Spirit; for the Spirit searches all things, even the depths of God.*[9]

When we give ourselves to the task of approaching the Scriptures with both *microscopic* and *telescopic* thinking, we allow the Holy Spirit to highlight the *details* of the text and at the same time give us a fresh perspective on things that lie in the *distance* – the promises that bring God's ultimate into our immediate.

TO *SPEAK* PROPHETICALLY YOU FIRST NEED TO *SEE* PROPHETICALLY

Enjoying the Journey

So, the journey of discovery has begun. The spark of an idea has started us on a preparatory process of *thinking, reading, meditating, researching, writing,* and *sketching* out rough ideas. And while this takes a serious amount of time, we should learn to enjoy the journey as much as the destination. Be warned, however. Time spent in preparing a sermon will invade your privacy and mess with your social life. People might accuse you of becoming somewhat distant. Leaving the party early, turning

[9] 1 Corinthians 2:10, NASB

down socialising opportunities, looking after your health, getting enough sleep, all these are part of the balanced lifestyle needed to become the best version of you. But those who appreciate and understand their high calling will willingly pay the price. Preaching God's Word is not some part-time, mediocre activity, something we do as a sideshow to the main event. It is our reason for being. It is the main event.

ANYONE WITH A MEASURE OF CHARISMA AND A NATURAL ABILITY FOR PUBLIC SPEAKING CAN WING IT

In your preparatory groundwork, keep the goal in view. I operate a say-it-in-one-sentence philosophy. I know when I am perfectly prepared and ready to preach when I give an elevator pitch. Let's say I meet someone in an elevator who asks me what I am planning to share. If in one sentence I can explain the content and purpose of my talk, and if the listener finds it easy to understand and interesting, I have done half the job!

Exercising single-mindedness, proclaimers of God's Word become thoroughly overwhelmed with the purpose of God in the message they are about to bring. Whether they *stumbled* on it or *searched* for it, they have found the treasure in the field and the pearl of great price and are willing to sacrifice their time and energy to cherish it, even if this means separating themselves for a season of prayerful study. They know that the personal expense will reap a spiritual reward.

Moving Beyond the Margins

We are living in a consumeristic society in which our surroundings are totally different from anything previous generations have witnessed. Our culture is constantly changing. Faced with this reality, would-be preachers are going to have to learn how to *Move Beyond the Margins.* In this, I am not advocating the removal of the ancient landmarks of biblical absolutes. I am saying that this is not the time to get stuck in the religious ruts of previous generations.

> **PROPHETIC PREACHERS ARE PACE-SETTERS WHO ENABLE OTHERS TO GET UP TO SPEED WITH THE PURPOSES OF GOD**

Situated within this present timeframe, we can either become *Smoke Detectors* or *Fire Extinguishers.* The first simply warn of the problem, whereas the second offer a viable solution. Put another way, we can either be *thermometers* or *thermostats.* The first measures the temperature in the room while the second changes the environment. As preachers, we cannot merely comment on a problem; we have to offer people a godly solution. We cannot merely take the temperature of what is going on around us; we need to exercise our God-given authority to change the environment. This is not a time to be tentative; it is a moment in history to take godly risks and preach in response to revelation, not intimidation.

WHILE SOME PREACHERS COMMENT ON SOCIETY, OTHERS SEEK TO CHANGE IT

It took a Moses to break Israel out of the confinement of Egypt, a Joshua to bring the *church in the wilderness* into the Promise Land, and a King David to fully establish God's kingdom on the earth. Right now, Christianity needs preachers who see God's larger purpose and will, by God's grace, *Move Beyond the Margins.* The big question is, "Will you dedicate yourself to becoming one of those for whom the activity of preaching will take people by the hand and enable them to reach beyond their present limitations into all that God has in store for them?" To look forward with the eye of faith, not to what the church has ever been, but to what it has never been.

Popeye Syndrome

Most genuine preachers will suffer from what I call the Popeye Syndrome. Driven by a *holy irritant,* these passionate individuals are totally consumed by the purpose of God. They willingly stand on the line for a heavenly cause, so much so that when the spinach moment comes they find themselves internally declaring, "That's all I can stands, 'cause I can't stands no more." Unable to stay silent, their goal is to create and deliver a transformative sermon that will challenge people and change the atmosphere.

Becoming righteously annoyed by what is happening around them, prophetic preachers cannot stand idly by and say nothing. They have seen beyond the veiled façade of human pretence into the supernatural realm. They have spent quality time studying the Scriptures and are fully prepared to deliver what they have received. This they will do with passion and a zeal birthed out of revelatory truth. Seeing what no one else is seeing, they say what no one else is saying.

DRIVEN BY A HOLY ANNOYANCE, GENUINE PREACHERS DRAW ON GOD'S GRACE TO DECLARE TRUTH AND BRING CHANGE

Discussion Points

- How do you see yourself in terms of moving beyond the margins?

- What is creating a "Holy Annoyance" in you right now?

- Do you see yourself as a detail or a distance person?

6
MAKE AN INVESTMENT

Established in 1929, the Boat Race is a rowing contest between two of the world's oldest universities – Oxford and Cambridge. It is advertised as "the world's longest surviving sporting challenge". This gruelling four-and-a-quarter-mile race demands the stamina of a marathon runner and the guts of a prize fighter. Each full-time university student commits to six months of blood, sweat, and tears for the chance to compete in an annual rowing race lasting about seventeen minutes. Mark de Rond spent a whole year observing the Cambridge squad and described this battle royal as "a race marked by 'tribal rivalry', and measured by a 'deep mutual respect' . . . It is all about taking part . . . yet the pain of losing is unimaginable".

What might seem a strange sporting ritual to some has for others become an

AS FORWARD-FACING THINKERS, PREACHERS STEER AND CHEER OTHERS

unmissable pre-Easter British event. Harnessing the incoming tide of the Thames River, each nine-man crew uses slim, carbon fibre-reinforced plastic racing boats known as *shells*. About these crew members, de Rond writes, "Eight of these are caught up in one of the most painful endurance sports imaginable for 4 miles and 374 yards on a whimsical, coffee-coloured course; for rowing requires not just cardiovascular fitness but enormous will-power to be able to push oneself through successive pain barriers . . . until one of [the crews] decides it can no longer win."[1]

While 80 per cent of the race depends on an eight-man crew, the remaining 20 per cent is down to choosing the right person to take the role of "cox" or "coxswain". Although their value is often underrated, a good cox can make or break a team. Facing waves, bitter winds, and tidal influences, the cox's seat is not for the faint-hearted. Within a stretch of fast water barely wide enough for the two boats to run side-by-side, each team fights for pole position around three large bends in the river. In

[1] Mark de Rond, *The Last Amateurs: To Hell and Back with the Cambridge Boat Race Crew* (Icon Books, 2008)

such challenging waters, the cox "has to recognise what is going wrong, why, and how it can be put right".[2] While controlling a rudder the size of a credit card, this person must find the fastest part of the river while negotiating a way forward that neither hinders nor helps the opposition.

Maintaining the necessary rhythm of all eight oarsmen, the cox is required to have the heart of a cheerleader and the spirit of a coach. The skill required is one which requires bringing the best out of people. Using diplomacy, empathy, and assertion, this forward-focused individual encourages each member of the crew – from the number one "stroke" who is setting the pace, to the "bow" man whose blades make the most difference – to go all out for the win. In this great endeavour, the cox uses words that coax, coach, motivate and, when necessary, calm each person as they strive for excellence.

PROPHETIC PREACHERS BRING THE BEST OUT OF PEOPLE

The cox's role during the race can be reduced to two basic requirements, to *steer* and *cheer* eight oarsmen to the finish line. As the only forward-facing person in the boat,

[2] Mark de Rond, *The Last Amateurs*

he or she has eight crew members looking to them for inspirational words of encouragement. The words they speak will carry the crew through to the finishing line.

But who encourages and directs the cox? How does this solitary person manage to care for, coach, and motivate themselves? How, when they are called to steer and cheer others, do they invest time and energy in their own personal welfare?

CONSTANTLY FACING THE CROWD AND ENCOURAGING OTHERS, PREACHERS NEED TO FIND A WAY TO INVEST IN THEMSELVES

"The way in which a leader conducts his personal life does, in fact, have a profound impact on [their] ability to exercise effective public leadership. There is a direct correlation between self-leadership and public leadership."[3] Within the pressure cooker of public speaking, it is easy to find yourself always giving and never receiving. The toughest management test preachers face is the ability to manage themselves. What are you doing to invest in your own well-being? Is your pace sustainable in the long-term? In a frantic life of steering and cheering others, you need constantly to consider how you manage to maintain a life lived in line with the

[3] Samuel D. Rima, *Leading From the Inside Out: The Art of Self Leadership* (Grand Rapids: Baker Books, 2007)

rhythms of grace? Remember what Jesus said. *Are you tired? Worn out? Burned out on religion? Come to me. Get away with me and you'll recover your life. I'll show you how to take a real rest. Walk with me and work with me – watch how I do it. Learn the unforced rhythms of grace. I won't lay anything heavy or ill-fitting on you. Keep company with me and you'll learn to live freely and lightly.*[4]

Waiting for My Soul to Catch Up

At the height of British colonialism, an English traveller arrives in Africa determined to get to his destination as quickly as possible. He charters some local porters to carry his supplies. After an exhausting day of travel, all on foot, and a fitful night's sleep, he gets up to continue the journey. But the porters refuse. Exasperated, he begins to cajole, bribe, plead, but nothing works. They will not move an inch. Naturally, he asks why. The answer is revealing. "They are waiting for their souls to catch up with their bodies."[5]

Following a hectic work schedule, Jesus would often call timeout.

THE BEST PREACHERS INVEST IN THEIR PHYSICAL, MENTAL AND SPIRITUAL WELL-BEING

[4] Matthew 11:28-30, MSG esp. v. 30
[5] John Mark Comer, *The Ruthless Elimination of Hurry* (Hodder & Stoughton, 2019)

Separating Himself from the pressing demands of a public ministry He would find the time and space to allow His soul to catch up with His body.

Constantly seeking to develop their calling, the best speakers are *self-investors*. The preachers and teachers we so greatly admire take the time to invest in their own physical, mental, and spiritual welfare. What, then, are we doing to invest in ourselves?

WHILE INVESTING IN OTHERS IS COMMENDABLE, INVESTING IN OURSELVES AS PREACHERS IS ESSENTIAL

There is a fascinating verse in Genesis that contains a directive from God to Abraham, or, as he was then known, Abram, "father of the faith". A citizen of a sophisticated society called Ur of the Chaldeans, Abram and his family were called by God to journey to a somewhat primitive land known as Canaan – a place *he was to receive for an inheritance.*[6] Integral to this call, is the command, *Go for yourself.*[7]

What does it mean to "go for yourself"?

Although to our highly spiritual senses this may sound like it contradicts the selfless life presented in the New Testament, there is a truth here. Within the life of total

[6] Hebrews 11:8, ESV
[7] Genesis 12:1, AMP

surrender, there is a place of personal preservation – a time to think about number one. Jesus knew the pressure of serving the crowds, but He managed to carve out time to rest and recuperate.[8] Finding time to invest in our mental, physical, spiritual, and emotional well-being is crucial for our long-term survival. Failing to do so is detrimental to our heavenly calling. Those forward-facing individuals called to steer and cheer others need to invest in their mental, physical, spiritual, and social well-being. Jesus was an investor who *kept increasing in wisdom and stature, and in favour with God and men.*[9] Where, then, do we need to focus our personal investment?

POOR PREACHING RESULTS FROM A LACK OF PERSONAL INVESTMENT

Energy

Tony Schwartz, one of the leading voices for energy management, talks of this technological age and how information is coming at us "faster and more relentless than ever". He then goes on to say that "unlike computers, however, human beings aren't meant to operate continuously, at high speeds, for long periods of time. Rather we're designed to move rhythmically". He

[8] Mark 6:31
[9] Luke 2:52, NASB

concludes by saying, "We live linear lives, progressively burning down our energy reservoirs throughout the day. It's the equivalent of withdrawing funds from a bank account without ever making a deposit. At some point, you go bankrupt."[10]

Although Schwartz is correct when he says that we all have much to learn about looking after our energy levels, as Christ followers we have an added life source – divine power. The apostle Paul had an amazing work ethic; he said, *I worked harder than all of them.*[11] Paul is continually portrayed as someone with exceptional energy levels. When writing to the Colossians he shares the secret of this life source:

Him [Christ] we proclaim, warning everyone and teaching everyone with all wisdom, that we may present everyone mature in Christ. For this I toil, struggling with all his ***energy*** *that he powerfully works within me.*[12]

Although common sense also tells us to give time and space for rest and recovery, to maintain a good diet and follow a regular exercise routine, as Christ followers we must never forget that we have God's

---

LEARN THE DIFFERENCE BETWEEN *THE ESSENTIAL YES* AND *THE NECESSARY NO!*

---

10 www.desiringgod.org/articles/god-will-give-you-the-energy
11 1 Corinthians 15:10
12 Colossians 1:28-29

energy . . . powerfully [working] within [us]. Knowing that certain people and events sap us of our strength, we need to learn how to manage our energy levels and recognise what rejuvenates us.

Whether a sporting activity, coffee with a mentor, a meal with friends, walking the dog, reading a great book, watching a good movie, or having shed time, whatever it is, be sure to invest quality time in those things that rejuvenate you. Besides investing in a balanced diet, physical exercise, regular health check-ups, and sufficient sleep, these things are crucial when it comes to managing your energy levels.

FIND OUT WHAT ENERGISES YOU, WHAT GIVES YOU A SPIRITUAL, PHYSICAL, AND EMOTIONAL BOOST, AND INVEST IN THOSE THINGS

Education

It can take up to ten years to train a doctor, seven a dentist, a minimum of five an architect. So, why is it we let preachers loose on a congregation with little formal or informal training? Jesus invested three years of 24/7 learning in a living room rather than a classroom setting and he did this to prepare His disciples before releasing them into a worldwide endeavour. The sink-or-swim philosophy that pushes would-be preachers in at the deep end is neither good nor godly. Is it any wonder that such poorly trained preachers often fall at the first huddle?

A WISE PREACHER KNOWS THE LONG-TERM RETURNS THAT COME FROM MAKING REGULAR SHORT-TERM INVESTMENTS

Treating learning as a personal investment, the best preachers give time and finance to becoming the best version of themselves. They are always reading, believing that those that read well, lead well. Never afraid to listen, or better still watch and listen, to their preaching endeavours, they are committed to a course of continuous personal improvement. Learning from their mistakes, they treat their failures as friends rather than intruders who come to silence their sense of calling. Without becoming too introspective, they examine their actions and look for ways to improve. They regularly press the pause button to rest and recuperate. Although it may seem a waste of time to others, those who invest in themselves have learned the personal benefits of self-regulation.

Experience

The Australian tennis player Rod Laver held his ranking as World

No. 1 for seven consecutive years and is the only tennis player to have twice won all four Grand Slam singles titles in the same year. Rated by some as the greatest male player of all time, Laver dominated world lawn tennis for more than a decade.

DON'T WAIT PASSIVELY FOR AN OPPORTUNITY TO PREACH; PREPARE YOURSELF NOW FOR WHAT YOU BELIEVE IS COMING FURTHER DOWN THE TRACK

Rod Laver owed much of his success to the expertise of his coach, Harry Christian Hopman. Harry had the uncanny skill of seeing and securing the very best in his players. In an effort to awaken the latent potential he had observed in young Rod, Harry nicknamed him "Rocket". A slow, short, scrawny-looking kid, Laver was anything but a rocket, yet Harry perceived potential and encapsulated it in the boy's new name. Some have suggested that Laver's nickname was given to counterbalance Laver's tendency to be lazy and inconsistent in using his inherent speed and agility. Whatever the truth, Harry's vision for Rod "Rocket" Laver helped turn this skinny kid into a spectacular sportsman who dominated the world of men's tennis during the early 1960s.

We all need a Harry in our life, a mentor who will unlock our hidden potential. Some may only be with us for a season, others for the long haul. Some may be up-close-and-personal, others may sharpen us from a distance. Whatever the context, these mentors help us become the best version of ourselves we can possibly be. Their example and expertise are invaluable. Realising that their personal development does not happened in isolation, self-investors therefore search for the guidance, wisdom, and knowledge of others. Feedback is the food of champions. Constructive input is therefore something worth seeking. Learning is for life.

WE ALL NEED MENTORS WHO WILL UNLOCK OUR UNREALISED POTENTIAL

Attending conferences, reading books, listening to podcasts, reading a blog are all things that will potentially improve our public-speaking skills. But the personal coaching of others is priceless for any would-be preachers. They are constantly looking for people they can spend time with and from whom they can learn, unafraid of taking time out to reflect on what God has called them to do.

Self-investors therefore willingly place themselves in situations that give them every opportunity to grow. Knowing that they are going to be stretched in such contexts will only serve to give them a greater capacity for a bigger future. They move beyond the margins of the familiar. Although scary, doing things they have never done before becomes more important than succumbing to the fear such challenges produce.

Take responsibility for your future because there are three kinds of people in the world. As the saying goes, there are those who watch things happen, those who make things happen, and those who ask what just happened. What new experiences are you planning? What new places are you going to visit?

IF YOU ARE SERIOUS ABOUT THE CALL OF GOD ON YOUR LIFE, THERE ARE BOOKS TO READ, PEOPLE TO CALL, AND PLACES TO GO

Environment

If there is one item of furniture whose loss future generations will mourn, it's the family dining table. Researchers tell us that if you are the kind of family that regularly sits around a meal table, you are in the minority. Young couples would rather buy the latest television than a dining table. Jewish tradition tells us that the table was a meeting place, an opportunity to share important things, a place where people sacrificed time to strengthen relationships, a place where family members found sustenance. The table creates an environment in which you can hear words that will help to push you forward in the journey of life.

PREACHERS NEED A QUIET PLACE, A STUDY ZONE WHERE WE CAN ENJOY SOLITUDE AND THE CHANCE TO THINK

What has table time to do with looking out for ourselves?

Everything!

Every preacher needs a desk to read, study, meditate. For some, this may prove challenging. If that's you, maybe start out with a table and a bookshelf in the corner of your bedroom. If it's at all possible, create a study area, better still a room, a place you can *go into . . . shut the door and pray.*[13]

Fortunately, during most of my preaching career I have had the privilege of having a dedicated study. In that well-lit room, I am surrounded with a large library of books collected over many years. I have a desk filled with mementoes, a comfortable chair, and some means of playing recorded music.

Whether on a tablet or in your hand, begin to build a personal

[13] Matthew 6:5–6; 2 Kings 4:33

library, tools to help you in the preparatory process of creating a sermon. In my own version of Desert Island Books, I would want to take:

1. Bible, NASB translation
2. Oxford English Dictionary
3. Strong's Concordance
4. Thayer's Greek-English Lexicon
5. Gesenius' Hebrew-Chaldee Lexicon
6. Notebook and writing implement
7. *The Shadow of the Almighty,* Elisabeth Elliot
8. *The Return of the Prodigal Son,* Henri J.M. Nouwen[14]

ALTHOUGH GOOGLE HAS REMOVED THE NEED FOR LARGE LIBRARIES, I AM SOMEONE WHO STILL LOVES THE TACTILE NATURE OF BOOKS

The Best Investment

As forward-facing people called to cheer and steer others, the best preachers and teachers have learned to invest in themselves. While ministering to others, they find the time and space to manage their *energy* levels, deepen their *education,* broaden their *experience,* and create a restful study *environment.* They, more than most, understand the

14 This is my personal list. Greek and Hebrew Lexicons are only useful if the student can correctly interpret them. A little knowledge is a dangerous thing.

thoughts behind E.C.W. Boulton's ancient hymn, "Move Me Dear Lord":

> O teach me, Lord, henceforth with Thee to walk in union deep; whilst tending other souls **not to neglect my own to keep;** a separated soul unto the One whose grace and love for me so much have done.

IT IS TIME TO LEARN HOW TO LET OUR SOULS CATCH UP WITH OUR BODIES.

The person who appreciates what God has invested in them will find time, make space, and spend finance to invest in themselves. As billionaire investor Warren Buffett says, "There's one investment that supersedes all others: Invest in yourself. Address whatever you feel your weaknesses are, and do it now. I was terrified of public speaking when I was young. I couldn't do it. It cost me $100 to take a Dale Carnegie course, and it changed my life. I got so confident about my new ability, I proposed to my wife during the middle of the course. It also helped me sell stocks in Omaha, despite being 21 and looking even younger. Nobody can take away what you've got in yourself—and everybody has potential they haven't used yet."[15] Whatever we do in terms of personal investment will pay dividends in the public arena.

15 https://www.forbes.com/sites/randalllane/2017/09/20/warren-buffett-my-greatest-investing-advice-and-the-investments-everyone-should-make/?sh=50169250593e

Discussion Points

- What does "allowing your soul time to catch up with your body" look like?

- How do you plan to invest in your future education?

- What does a productive study environment mean for you?

- What is the perfect scenario for increasing your spiritual experience?

BAIT THE HOOK 7

My father taught me many things; he gave me a love for woodwork and all things automobile related. He also gifted me with a passion for fishing. Being a businessman with little time to spare, some of the most memorable moments we spent together were on the banks of various lakes. Having supplied me with the basics, he patiently showed me how to thread a line, choose a float, and attach a hook. He pointed out the best places to fish and how to cast a line and land a fish. Perhaps the most important lesson of all was how to *Bait the Hook*. Besides making and throwing ground bait, my dad showed how to attach either a worm, maggot, morsel of bread, or piece of cheese to the hook. The life lesson was this: you can have the most expensive equipment, the most idyllic location, and the most skilled mentor possible, but without the correct bait you have little chance of catching anything.

The same can be said of sermon preparation. You can collect an endless supply of preaching manuals, listen to the best orators, and learn from the best mentors the basic mechanics and dynamics of preaching, but unless you learn how to bait the hook you have little chance of catching, let alone sustaining, anyone's attention.

A LACK OF VERBAL CONTINUITY WILL UNDOUBTEDLY AFFECT A LISTENER'S CONNECTIVITY

If, like me, you are the kind of person who never reads the instruction manual before attempting to build a flat-packed piece of furniture, then this chapter might prove a little challenging. Preaching is not a career choice; it's a divine calling. This call involves allowing the Holy Spirit to craft both the individual and the sermon in both the preparation and the presentation of a message. What at first might seem a little tedious is crucial. To craft any talk takes time; you need to weave thoughts, ideas, illustrations into a verbal garment that others will wear. For those too casual and unconcerned to follow this process, what they present in public is liable to be a shambolic mess.

Giving a Structure to Your Message

Having embraced the spark of an idea, and begun the preparatory process of praying, thinking, reading, researching, writing and sketching out some rough ideas, it's now time to begin to construct a written framework, a structure that will support your overall message.

Steve Jobs created presentations that were "very much a dramatic play – a finely designed and well-rehearsed performance that informs, entertains, and inspires".[1] The importance of designing a good structure cannot be overstated. It is this structure that will become the roadmap, the GPS, that guides your listener to a clear conclusion and a call to action. Rush this part of the process and you run the risk of creating a talk that is unready and unfit for purpose.

IF OUR SERMONS ARE TO BE TRANSFORMATIVE, THEY WILL NEED SHAPE AND STRUCTURE

In the task of creating a viable structure for a public speech, consider the Greek philosopher Aristotle's five ingredients needed to persuade an audience:

1. Create a STORY that arouses

[1] Carmine Gallo *The Presentation Secrets of Steve Jobs*

the audience's interest

2. Raise a PROBLEM that must be solved

3. Offer a SOLUTION to the problem raised

4. Describe the BENEFITS for adopting the course of action

5. State a call to ACTION. What do you want your audience to do?[2]

"GOOD SERMONS ARE LIKE A GOOD MOVIE OR GOOD BOOK. THEY ENGAGE YOU FROM THE BEGINNING BY CREATING SOME KIND OF TENSION."

"Good sermons are like good movies or a good book. They engage you at the beginning by creating some kind of tension. They resolve that tension. There is a climax. And then there is a conclusion that ties up all the loose ends. Pretty simple. When you can reduce your message to a few big pieces it will read like a story. It will be memorable like a movie."[3]

Some people think of three essential elements when considering the structure of a sermon. Using the simple idea of a menu, they have the *starter*, the *main course*, and the *dessert*. But this puts too much emphasis on the main meal. At the risk of mixing metaphors, a better analogy is that of an aeroplane journey, with the *take-off* – or introduction – and the

2 www.edisonred.com/media/15278/Aristotle_5
3 Andy Stanley and Lane Jones, *Communicating for a Change*

landing – or conclusion. The time spent between those two vital points is the *in-flight journey*.

Just as the skeletal system gives shape and structure to the human body, so a sermon is strengthened and supported by its overall framework. The structure holds everything in place and brings life and movement. This means that the initial flash of inspiration and the rough ideas we have been sketching must now find their form. The beginning, middle, and end are like a three-ply thread; although woven together to create a strong, coherent, beautiful message, each part is crucial to the whole.

IT IS THE SHAPE AND STRUCTURE OF A SERMON THAT WILL SUPPORT THE SINGLE THEME WHICH THE HOLY SPIRIT IS ASKING YOU TO SHARE

The Landing

Although it might sound strange to begin with the conclusion, all preachers need to know their end point before they begin their journey. Once a pilot knows their destination, everything else will fit into place. To use yet another metaphor, like a musical masterpiece moving towards a crescendo, all sermons should work towards a perceived and well-planned conclusion. Without this, we run the risk of creating a cacophony of sounds that lacks sense or sequence. Every staging post within a sermon is leading towards this climactic moment. If you do not know where you are heading, how do you expect the listener to journey with you?

PREACHING WITHOUT A MENTAL ROUTE MAP RUNS THE RISK OF BECOMING A VERBAL RAMBLE

While the trip might prove enjoyable, the point of the whole exercise will be lost in the wasteful wandering. Learning to land your talk is something all would-be preachers need to practise and perfect.

Ask yourself this question: what if the listener was to leave your sermon halfway through? Would they later wish they had stayed to the end? The conclusion is more than bringing closure to your message. It is the culmination of hours of prayerful preparation, and as such deserves careful consideration.

Just as a pilot is required to give 100 per cent attention to *take-off* and *landing* – with the option of engaging the autopilot during the *in-flight journey* – so a sermon's conclusion requires a considerable amount of concentration. The closing remarks should hold high-status value in the preacher's mind. By using a poignant story, a vibrant quotation, or a series of questions, the *landing* needs to include an application and a clear call to action, [more of this under *Order a Takeaway*]. It should cause the listener to consider how they are going to apply the biblical truth they have just heard. Co-working with the Holy Spirit, the preacher needs to pray that the listener is so convinced and convicted that they are willing to make necessary changes in the piercing light of the truth you have shared.

A good *landing* – as opposed to a bumpy one – will always involve:

- Restating the main theme
- Summarising the journey
- Making a clear and final application
- Calling for a response

Finally, please remember that the conclusion should conclude. Conclusions are not the opportunity for protracting your talk, prevaricating, or procrastinating. If you promise to end, end!

PREACHERS SHOULD PICTURE THEIR DESTINATION BEFORE PLANNING THEIR JOURNEY

The Take-off

All would-be preachers are well advised to work hard at crafting their introductory comments. "You have at most 3-5 minutes to capture your congregation's interest – or the next 20 are spent fighting to bring them back again. Your introduction will either capture or lose them."[4] Take-off and landing are the bookends of a transformative experience. As Haddon W. Robinson writes, "During the introduction, an audience gains impressions of a speaker that often determine whether or not they will accept what he says. If he appears nervous, hostile, or unprepared, they are inclined to reject him. If he seems alert, friendly, and interesting, they decide he is an able person with a positive attitude towards himself and his listeners."[5]

BY BAITING THE HOOK, WE CREATE A LURE THAT ATTRACTS THE LISTENER TO COME CLOSER

In my opinion, a preacher has a few brief moments in which to either engage or disengage their listeners. In that moment in time when a preacher is inviting people to get on board, the importance of *baiting the hook* well cannot be overstated. It is here that the speaker finds common ground with their

4 Bryn Jones, *Homiletics* Seminar
5 Haddon W. Robinson, *Biblical Preaching* (Baker Academic, 2017)

listeners. By presenting a tension that resonates with the listener, the preacher begins a journey to find God's answer. If the speaker fails to declare the purpose of their talk in an engaging way, people will begin to leave the room mentally, if not physically. An engaging *take-off* will make all the difference, so why not consider *baiting the hook* with the following:

- A personal dilemma that resonates with the listener
- An engaging title
- A great quote
- A serious or humorous story
- An action that requires a mental reaction – maybe a non-responsive question

PREACHERS HAVE A FEW MOMENTS IN WHICH TO ENGAGE OR DISENGAGE THEIR LISTENERS

Although we have not touched on the issue of notes, some speakers feel that the *take-off* and *landing* are so important they write them out in full text – if only to then memorise them. Their *in-flight journey* may just have bullet points. My preferred method is to write the whole sermon out word-for-word. Anyone could pick up my notes and read them from beginning to end. Although not advocating we read our sermons, I would rather memorise the text and only refer to my notes as a point of reference.

WHAT ARE THE *STICKY STATEMENTS* THAT MAKE YOUR TALK MEMORABLE?

The In-flight Journey

As in any long-haul flight this is the period between *take-off* and *landing* when those travelling with you are prone to switching off. With that in mind careful consideration needs to be given to questions like:

• What is the *one thing* I want to say and how will I say it?

• What are the essential elements of this talk?

• What are my main points with which I will journey the listener and make this sermon flow in a flawless manner?

• How will I transition from the take-off to my first point through each subsequent point to the eventual landing?

• What are the "sticky statements"[6] that make the talk memorable and help people to remember the central theme of this talk?

[6] Andy Stanley and Lane Jones, *Communicating for a Change*

Although your nerves may tempt you to do otherwise, you should periodically scan your audience. Avoid fixing your eyes only on those people who you know will boost your confidence. Most gatherings will have a mixture of ages, cultures, and educational abilities. It is important to know if your words are connecting with people from diverse backgrounds.

YOUR MAIN POINTS FORM THE SCAFFOLDING THAT HOLDS THE STRUCTURE OF YOUR SERMON TOGETHER

Benjamin Zander, the conductor of the Boston Philharmonic Orchestra, calls this process "looking for shining eyes". As he trains singers and musicians to perform to an audience, he encourages them to see if their music or song is resonating with those listening. For a preacher, this means scanning a congregation to check if your words are finding a positive response in the hearts of your listeners? The lack of either a visible or verbal response does not always mean that people are not listening. Some people are simply assimilating the truth in a non-verbal, non-observable manner. This is especially the case when preachers are speaking to more reserved English audiences!

If a lack of response is because

people are struggling to understand your argument, then you should be prepared to insert a story to illustrate your point and regain their interest. However, remember that an illustration is a window that allows light to illuminate a darkened understanding. Avoid "the greenhouse effect" in which your whole sermon is nothing more than a series of stories with no biblical content whatsoever.

PREACHERS DON'T JUST SAY SOMETHING; THEY HAVE SOMETHING TO SAY

Preaching Styles

If preaching is best defined as "truth via personality",[7] then God takes a variety of personalities through which to communicate His truth. None of the following styles is either right or wrong. The important task is to *Be Yourself, Find Your Voice,* and let the Holy Spirit do the rest. We need to identify what it means to be "naturally supernatural" and let the Holy Spirit make us channels through which the truth flows. Being who we really are will prevent us from becoming a façade, a facsimile of what God has intended for our lives.

Consider the following preaching

[7] Based on Phillips Brooks' *Lectures on Preaching* in which he defines preaching as "communication of truth through personality".

styles and consider which may apply to you.[8]

The Artist

The preacher-as-artist is the person who paints (in words) on a large canvas for their listeners. Using big brush strokes, they are rarely concerned with detail. They keep verbally painting until the listener sees the picture come to life. By the time they have reached the conclusion, they have somehow managed to paint the listener into their landscape. The listener becomes the woman with the blood condition pressing through the crowd just to touch the corner of Christ's prayer shawl.

THE ARTIST-PREACHERS HELPS THE LISTENER TO PLACE THEIR STORY WITHIN THE BIG STORY

The Actor

Actors have vivid imaginations. They don't just talk about David facing Goliath; they become David. They do not worry what people think about them. Using the whole stage, they often use props – anything that will help them visually act out the biblical scene. They will pull on every human emotion to introduce the listener to the risen, glorified Christ.

[8] *Homiletics* – these seven styles of preaching are accredited to the notes from a seminar conducted by Bryn Jones in 1985. Used with permission.

WHILE THE BIOLOGIST DISSECTS THE TEXT THE HAMMER & NAILS PREACHER DRIVES EVERY POINT HOME

The Biologist

The Biologist dissects every part of the text. They cut a particular verse into single words and then subdivide the words into their component parts, tracing each word back to its original meaning. When the right person does this, it can be a joy. Done by the wrong person, it can prove disastrous. If it is not anointed, it can prove painful. Expository preaching (the style of "the biologist") is very analytical and requires anointed preparation and presentation.

Hammer and Nails Person

Such preachers may have numerous points to make, but each one is hammered home. Using tweetable phrases, they repeat the same point in a variety of ways. Every time they do, people feel it. If someone is given this skill to speak, it will cause people to sit up and listen. However, in the hands of the unskilled practitioner, it can come across as "Bible-thumping".

The Spider's Web

In this style of preaching, the speaker creates a net in which the listener becomes increasingly ensnared. Without realising what is happening, they are drawn further and further into the argument until suddenly they are caught. Evangelistic in purpose, this is the style Jesus used with the woman at the well in John 4, and with the woman caught in adultery in John 8.

THE EVANGELIST BILLY GRAHAM WAS A SKILFUL PRACTITIONER OF *THE SPIDER'S WEB* APPROACH.

The Newscaster

The Newscaster gives the listener a fast commentary on life, not as an artist or an actor, but as an observer. Using up-to-date stories, quotations, facts, and research details, they take the listener on a fact-finding journey. The newscaster causes the audience to become fascinated and intrigued. Before they know it, they have arrived at a predetermined destination and people are making a commitment to follow Christ.

The Schoolteacher

These preachers develop a logical argument through various points, each one springing from the other with impact. The advantage of this style is it keeps the focus of the objective clear. While some preachers lose their way and start waffling, the schoolteacher is too well organised to do that. The schoolteacher builds their argument one layer on top of another, each layer adding a new dimension on a stairway to heavenly realities.

Try to recognise where you think you fit within this list of characters. "If you're new to teaching and preaching, your communication style may yet be incubating."[9] If preaching is truth via personality, there will be some natural character traits that God will seek to develop in you. It is possible that you are a mixture of more than one of these different preaching characters. By identifying your preferred style, you can look to the Holy Spirit to develop your ministry more perfectly.

***MAKING THE MUMMIES DANCE* CAN ONLY HAPPEN WHEN YOU CREATE A TRANSFORMATIONAL EXPERIENCE FOR YOUR LISTENERS**

[9] Dave Stone, *Refining Your Style: Learning from Respected Communicators* (Group Publishing, 2004)

Discussion Points

- What is the purpose of a good take-off?

- What is the most difficult part of the sermon journey – from take-off to landing?

- Which preaching style are you most drawn to and why?

8
ENJOY THE JOURNEY

The 1980s movie *Clockwise* reminds me of the days that typically run up to a preaching engagement. It stars the inimitable John Cleese. He plays the part of a secondary school headteacher called Brian Stimpson who oversees a 1980s comprehensive school. In stark contrast to the chaos of his own teenage years, Stimpson is obsessed with organisation, punctuality, order, and discipline. He runs his school like "clockwork".

In recognition of his successful headship, Stimpson is selected to bring a keynote speech to the annual headmasters' conference in the city of Norwich. An honour normally reserved for heads from elite public schools, Stimpson is the first headmaster from a comprehensive school to be offered this prestigious opportunity.

In true Stimpson style, he rehearses

his speech repeatedly. However, his regimentally organised travel arrangements begin to go horribly awry when he boards the wrong train. In the rush to change trains, he accidently leaves his notes behind. His dream appointment is fast becoming a horrible nightmare. Through a series of misadventures, Stimpson's ordered world begins to unravel.

SERMON PREPARATION IS A JOURNEY TO ENJOY NOT A CHORE TO ENDURE

Things go from bad to worse when Stimpson fails to locate his wife who is supposed to drive him to his appointment. His failure to hail a taxi leads him to coerce a sixth-form student (playing truant during a study break) to drive him in her parents' car to the conference. In the final scenes, a dishevelled headteacher, Stimpson's wife, police officers investigating reports of a stolen car, and a vehicle full of dementia patients from the local hospital are all seen in pursuit of headmaster Stimpson – a colourful climax to a nightmare journey.

Clockwise portrays a parallel to the days that can run up to a preaching appointment. Whatever is happening at work, home, or in the community, the preacher's mind is focused and fixated upon the task at hand. Within the difficulties, diversions, and distractions of everyday life, there is a perpetual reminder of a preaching appointment, the destination towards which they are travelling. Thoroughly overwhelmed with the purpose of God, every waking moment will be accompanied by mental rehearsal. Trial runs through the introduction, main body of the talk, and its conclusion become second nature. Driving to and from various appointments, walking the dog, cleaning the car, gardening, are all opportunities to have impromptu rehearsals.

THROUGH THE HIGHS AND LOWS OF A BUSY SCHEDULE, WOULD-BE PREACHERS REHEARSE THEIR MESSAGE IN WHATEVER OPPORTUNITY LIFE GIVES THEM

(1) The Joy of Discovery

In the fight against COVID-19, most people have rejoiced in the rollout of the University of Oxford AstraZeneca vaccine. The concerns some people have regarding its speedy development need to be kept in context. Long before the first infections were detected in Wuhan, China, scientists had been developing the basic platform on which this vaccine was going to be built. In the wake of the Ebola outbreak in 2014–2016, researchers began a journey of discovery that ultimately led to the development of a vaccine to combat COVID-19.

WHAT WE REJOICE IN TODAY IS OFTEN THE RESULT OF A DISCOVERY THAT HAS BEEN YEARS IN THE MAKING

When it came to Einstein's theory of relativity; Alexander Fleming's work with antibiotics, James Watson's and Francis Crick's unearthing of DNA, they all took time to bring their theories into reality. As proclaimers of God's Word, we likewise need to remember that transformative sermons require a journey of discovery.

After fifty years of preaching and teaching God's Word, I still get excited by the pursuit of godly understanding. There is little to compare with the joy when biblical research results in a *eureka* moment – that Holy Spirit-inspired revelation that makes you want to tell the world of a mind-blowing, ear-tingling, eye-opening, earth-shattering biblical truth.

Consider the journey of the two discouraged disciples making their way home to Emmaus. Having witnessed the death of their dream, everything changes as the risen Christ draws alongside them.

Looking back on this moment, they asked, *Didn't we feel on fire as he conversed with us on the road, as he opened up the Scriptures for us?* Bursting with the joy of their discovery, *They didn't waste a minute. They were up and on their way back to Jerusalem. They found the Eleven and their friends . . . "It's really happened! The Master has been raised up!"*[1] When in prayerful study God's Spirit draws alongside you to *guide you into all the truth,*[2] then your preaching becomes a Matthew 12:34 experience; *out of the abundance of the heart the mouth speaks.*[3]

WHAT IGNITES THE SPEAKER WILL SPARK INTEREST IN THE LISTENER

Stumbling on the Truth

Jesus spoke of the joy of this kind of discovery in the Parable of the Treasure in the Field and the Parable of the Pearl of Great Price.[4] The man ploughing the field was going about his everyday business when he happened to *stumble* on a treasure. A normal day became abnormal as he tripped over this previously hidden fortune. He may have worked the same field on numerous occasions, but today was different.

How often have we re-read a portion of Scripture only to stumble

[1] Luke 24:32, MSG
[2] John 16:13
[3] Matthew 12:34, NKJV
[4] Matthew 13:44–46

on something that we have never seen? The previously unseen is seen and the unknown known. In *his joy,* the finder is desperate to become the keeper. Selling *all that he has [he] buys that field.* He has no intention of stealing what belongs to another; he wants legitimately to own the treasure for himself.

ACCIDENTALLY TRIPPING OVER TRUTH HAPPENS MORE OFTEN THAN WE THINK

The joy of biblical discovery will do that to a person. Preachers, like ploughmen, often stumble upon kingdom treasures. When this happens, they become so overwhelmed with the purpose of heaven on earth that they willingly pay the price to buy into the truth. It is this ecstatic joy that should permeate a preacher's study time as they, with the Holy Spirit's help, unearth kingdom realities.[5]

Searching for Truth

The *merchant*[6] is also a person on a journey.[7] He is a dealer on a lifelong quest for *fine pearls.* Wholly consumed in a voyage of discovery, his quest is the *one pearl of great value.* Just like the ploughman, the pearl merchant is sold out for God's kingdom of *righteousness, peace and joy.*[8] Things of a lesser earthly value

[5] Matthew 16:16–20, Ephesians 1:17
[6] Matthew 13:45
[7] The literal meaning of the word "merchant" is "one on a journey".
[8] Romans 14:17

pale into insignificance in the light of that one and only pearl found in the person of Jesus Christ.

Preachers are spiritual journeymen and women on a lifelong quest to discover more of the person, power, and presence of a holy God. They are retailers who specialise in priceless pearls of heavenly wisdom. Partnering with the Holy Spirit, they are like the ancient prophets who *searched diligently*[9] for the grace of God. Like the wisemen who *search diligently*[10] for the Christ child, preachers search for God's truth. Believing the Scriptures contain priceless gems, their approach to biblical study is one of joyful expectation. They look to the Holy Spirit who *searches all things, even the depths of God*[11] to reveal those *things which eye has not seen.*[12]

FOR THE PREACHER, THE JOY OF DISCOVERY IS ONLY EQUALLED BY THE JOY OF DELIVERY

(2) The Joy of Delivery

Preachers love nothing more than to create a party atmosphere that celebrates what they themselves have found and would very much want others to find too. They are like honeybees returning to the hive after discovering a place of high pollen count. They tell their fellow

9 1 Peter 1:10, KJV
10 Matthew 2:8, KJV
11 1 Corinthians 2:10, NASB
12 1 Corinthians 2:9, NASB

bees the distance and direction they will need to travel to find the best nectar.

This is the essence of the trilogy of parables in Luke 15. Whether it is finding a lost sheep, a lost coin, or a lost son, the result is a party on earth mirroring the one in heaven. Preaching is a matter of sharing with others how to find what we have found, so that we can rejoice together in the goodness of God. This should be the goal of every sermon.

TRUE PREACHING CREATES A PARTY ATMOSPHERE IN WHICH OTHERS ENJOY THE DISCOVERY OF BIBLICAL TRUTH

What has taken hours to prepare, might only take a few minutes to share, but the joy of channelling God's truth to others is exhilarating. Preaching involves inviting others to join you in buying into the truth you have personally discovered. When that happens, heaven and earth join forces to enjoy a praise party that celebrates the risen, glorified Christ.

If you want to experience a greater degree of joy in the delivery, understand what it means to *Walk the Talk, Turn the Chair Around,* and to answer the question of *Notes or No Notes.* These are key issues when it comes to perfecting the art of preaching.

Walk the Talk

The most proficient preachers practise their delivery. They inwardly digest the message. They marinate themselves in the truth, so that when asked by a critical friend, they could share in a conversational manner the essence of their talk. Before ever stepping onto a platform or into a pulpit, do yourself a favour – speak your message to an empty room as you practise for the main event. Use every opportunity you have to run through your talk, driving to and from appointments, country walks, are all God-given opportunities to practise and perfect the art of preaching. By repeatedly rehearsing your talk, you give yourself time to become comfortable with your notes, words, turns of phrase, Scriptural references, key statements, stories, and any awkward biblical names. When you find areas that need adjustment, you still have time to add or subtract from the overall text.

PROFICIENT PREACHERS PRACTISE AND PERFECT THE ART OF PREACHING

This is a practice that began back in Bible college in England. I would frequent a disused airfield. From here, Spitfire pilots had engaged the enemy in numerous dogfights during the Battle of Britain. Some twenty years on, the remnants of earthworks marked the spots where they would park their aeroplanes. Looking at the grassy embankments, I imagined people seated on tiers as I began a journey that has lasted for over half of a century. In a disused World War II airfield, I first discovered what it meant to walk the talk.

PRACTISE WHAT YOU PREACH

When we engage in this part of our preparation, we should ask:

- Is the main theme the main thing?
- Will the hook engage people at the start?
- Is there sufficient Bible content?
- What do I need to add or remove from my text?
- Is my application clear?
- What will my listeners understand as the call to action?

Turn the Chair Around

Because you want people to get on the bus, learn to *Turn the Chair Around*. Put yourself in the listener's seat and listen to what you are saying from their perspective. Having spent time beforehand getting to knowing the social, cultural, spiritual, and fiscal mix of your listeners, ask yourself questions:

- Does this talk have common ground for those listening?
- Will the take-off empathise with people in a way that causes them to engage?
- Are my objectives clear?
- Will this message give me understanding that leads to spiritual growth?
- Is this message full of godly substance?
- Will this sermon flow flawlessly?
- Has this message had such an impact on my life that I would gladly listen to it again?

THE BEST PREACHERS VALUE CONTINUOUS IMPROVEMENT

Notes or No Notes

The ability to construct and deliver a transformative sermon that has clarity, beauty, imagination, passion, and humour will to a large degree depend on a preacher's notes.

Although all communicators use

notes, listeners should not be aware of them and speakers should not be tied to them. Adding further fuel to the fire Andy Stanley writes, "If an actor is willing to memorise and internalise a script in order to convince you that he or she is someone other than who they really are, how motivated should we be to internalise our message in order to convince our audience that we really are who we claim to be."[13]

A WELL-CONSTRUCTED SERMON IS OFTEN THE RESULT OF A WELL-ARRANGED SET OF NOTES.

Whether or not they are used, or the degree to which they are memorised and referred to, is a matter of personal preference. Having captured that flash of inspiration, you have prayerfully spent hours thinking, reading, researching, marinating in, and scribbling down a series of rough ideas. Now is the time to gather all that material into a set of usable notes which will aid you and the listener to journey together to a set destination.

Only in extreme circumstances should any would-be preacher talk without some form of written or typed framework they can follow. Although the style, structure, and substance of a speaker's notes are

13 Andy Stanley and Lane Jones, *Communicating for a Change*

personal, here are some helpful hints:

- How much detail you include is a matter of personal preference
- Writing Bible verses out in full is often helpful
- Use highlighter pens, capital letters, or colour codes to mark key points and phrases
- Do not cramp your notes and make them large enough to be readable
- Practise, practise, practise preaching with or without your notes[14]

The preparation and presentation of God's Word is a spiritual journey of discovery in which some speakers find *sermon mapping* a great help. This is a graphic representation of the contents of a speech that helps the speaker to visually track their progress. Laying their notes out like a literal map, they use arrows to mark their direction of travel. They signpost major points of interest. *Sermon mapping* provides the speaker with a starting point and a pre-determined destination and hopefully makes the whole journey a more enjoyable experience for

SERMON MAPPING PROVIDES THE SPEAKER WITH A STARTING POINT AND A PRE-DETERMINED DESTINATION

14 See also Francis Chan, *Seven Questions To Ask Before You Preach* (2019) www.sermoncentral.com

both the speaker and their listeners.

Those who struggle to find enjoyment in the role of public preaching should perhaps ask themselves if this is their God-given calling. Maybe you have inadvertently stepped into a realm for which you're not suited. Those able to teach individuals, groups, or classes may not necessarily be best for preaching to much larger groups on a Sunday. Being a type-two speaker in a type-three setting is painful both to the speaker and the listener. Whatever your fit, the sense of fulfilment and enjoyment in the preparation and presentation come from feeling that you are "in your zone". Life is too short to persistently practise something that brings no pleasure to you or God!

IF THERE IS NO PLEASURE IN THE PREPARATION, THERE IS UNLIKELY TO BE ANY IN THE PRESENTATION

We are either commentators or communicators. Whereas commentators rarely change anything, communicators do the following:

- Believe in what they say – CONVICTION
- Believe in the people they are saying it to – EXPECTATION

- Practise what they preach – CREDIBILITY
- Know when to say it – TIMING
- Know how to say it – CREATIVITY
- Know why they say it – APPLICATION
- Have fun saying it – ENJOYMENT
- Show it as they say it – VISUALISATION
- Say it and people own it – IDENTIFICATION
- Say it and people live it – ACTUALISATION

SOCIAL COMMENTATORS RARELY CHANGE ANYTHING

Discussion Points

- What aspects of your everyday life cause you problems when preparing to preach?

- What is your greatest challenge to public speaking?

- What enjoyment do you find in preparing and presenting a sermon?

FEEL THE BURN 9

English pageantry is renowned throughout the world and Trooping the Colour on London's Horse Guards Parade is perhaps British pomp and ceremony at its best. Military precision, horsemanship, fanfare, and soldiers in full ceremonial regalia are all present and correct to mark the Queen's official birthday. This colourful display of monarchy, music, and marching bands creates a magnificent spectacle.

When watching the mounted band of the Household Cavalry, even the most casual onlooker cannot help but be impressed by the drum horses. Senior to all army animals, they are ridden by the drummers. Steering the horses with reins attached to their feet, these soldiers exercise extraordinary horsemanship. Carrying two heavy, solid-silver kettle drums, the horses seem unfazed by the sights and sounds around them. The drum horse is truly one of the most recognisable and impressive of all creatures.

For me, this colourful parade offers a prophetic backdrop to the ongoing purposes of God. The drummer and the drum horse speak of those royally commissioned to preach God's Word. The two kettle drums represent the Word and the Spirit. What a royal privilege it is to be enlisted as someone whose task it is to echo the sounds of heaven on earth! What an honour to set the rhythm for the marching army of the Lord!

CHARISMATIC PREACHERS CAN BE A LIABILITY TO RECOVER FROM RATHER THAN A GOAL TO AIM FOR

Charismatic preachers can be colourful characters. As individuals who stand out from the crowd, they make their presence felt. However, their charisma can be a smokescreen for a flawed character. Natural orators, gifted communicators, and impressive wordsmiths they may be, but without the Word and the Spirit, they fail to set a prophetic tempo for the gathered assembly of God's people.

More than being keynote speakers, those called to preach must march to a different drumbeat. Impassioned by the purpose of God's Word and driven by the dynamics of God's

Spirit, they align themselves to the heartbeat of heaven.

One of the greatest expository preachers of the 20th century, Dr Martyn Lloyd-Jones, described preaching as "logic on fire".[1] When it is logic on fire, the act of preaching becomes a means of *Making the Mummies Dance.* Turning religious graveyards into resurrection cities, anointed proclaimers of truth awaken slumbering saints from their spiritual stupor. Speaking words of *Spirit and life,*[2] Spirit-filled preachers bring life-giving words to *corpses, dead in [their]sins and offences.*[3] The key here is the combination of Word and Spirit, of Scripture and the power of God. All Word and no Spirit may inform the mind but does little to regenerate the spirit. All Spirit and no Word may stir the senses but in the long term it will fail to bring knowledge, understanding, and spiritual growth, thereby creating a pastoral pandemic of problematic and immature believers unable to apply biblical truth to their everyday lives.

PREACHING BECOMES EFFECTIVE WHEN THERE IS AN INTERACTION BETWEEN GOD'S WORD AND SPIRIT

The famous Baptist preacher W.A. Criswell puts it this way: "The Sermon is no essay to be read

[1] Dr Martyn Lloyd-Jones, *Preachers and Preaching*
[2] John 6:63
[3] Ephesians 2:1, TPT

for optional opinion, for people to casually consider. It is confrontation with Almighty God. It is to be delivered with a burning passion, in the authority of the Holy Spirit."[4]

LIFELESS SERMONS AND LISTLESS PREACHERS WILL DO LITTLE TO CREATE AN ENVIRONMENT IN WHICH THE MUMMIES DANCE

Feel the Burn

My message and my preaching, wrote the apostle Paul, *were not in persuasive words of wisdom, but in demonstration of the Spirit and of power.* Paul reminded us that *the kingdom of God is not a matter of talk but of power.*[5] Elsewhere he said, *our gospel came to you not simply with words but also with power, with the Holy Spirit and deep conviction.*[6] It is *the living Word of God, which is full of energy,*[7] delivered by Spirit-filled preachers, that will open the graves of unbelief and doubt. Exercising godly authority, they breathe life where there is spiritual death.

We stand at a pivotal moment in history when God is seeking to raise an army of preachers – a spiritual force marching to a different drumbeat. God is looking for preachers who will deliver life-giving sermons, Bible teachers who will call people, like Lazarus, to

[4] Alex Montoya, *Preaching with Passion* (Kregel Publications, 2000)
[5] 1 Corinthians 2:4; 4:20, NASB
[6] 1 Thessalonians 1:5
[7] Hebrews 4:12, TPT

come forth from the grave and be loosed from the bands of death.

It is said that when Abraham Lincoln experienced dark emotional moments he would often walk over to his local church and listen to the preaching of Dr Gurley. Time had taught him that listening to the pastor's inspired sermons gave him wise counsel.

THE WORLD NEEDS ANOINTED PREACHERS DELIVERING LIFE-GIVING SERMONS

"On a particular Wednesday evening, the melancholy Lincoln and an aide slipped quietly into a pew near the back of the sanctuary of the church and listened to Dr Gurley's midweek message. Afterwards Lincoln and his aide made their way back along Pennsylvania Avenue. To break the silence of the night, the aide asked the President a question. 'Did you like Dr Gurley's sermon tonight, Mr President?' 'No,' came Lincoln's direct reply. 'It was a failure, so far as I was concerned.' 'Why do you say that, sir? Was it the content or the structure that you did not like?' 'The content was as fine as ever for Dr Gurley,' said Lincoln. 'And the structure was good too. The sermon was a failure because Dr Gurley missed a glorious opportunity to stir us to rise and do something great for Christ."[8]

Old Testament prophets were *men [who] spoke from God, [those] who were borne along (moved and impelled) by the Holy Spirit.*[9] The original Hebrew word for *prophet* is related to the idea of *bubbling up.* The prophets acted like an ancient Artesian well in which their words *bubbled* up from a subterranean life source deep in their innermost being. Jeremiah spoke of this spiritual dynamic when he said, *[God's] word is in my heart [burning] like a fire, a fire shut up in my bones.*[10] Other prophets spoke of the responsibility of proclaiming the truth as a *burden.*[11] Those called to preach will experience the fire of a *burning* passion because the Holy Spirit must first consume the preacher before igniting the listener. Like celebratory champagne, God's Word will *bubble up* from deep within the one called to preach. As those who represent heaven's interests on earth, the responsibility of declaring God's Word will also at times be a weighty *burden.*

PREACHING IS A GLORIOUS OPPORTUNITY TO STIR PEOPLE TO DO SOMETHING GREAT FOR JESUS

Fuel Your Passion

I am a child of the sixties and the

8 Preaching.com/restoring-our-passion-for-excellence-in-preaching/
9 2 Peter 1:21, AMP
10 Jeremiah 20:9
11 Malachi 1:1, KJV

first lunar landing is one of my lasting memories. Those who lived through this historic event will know exactly where they were and what they were doing when Neil Armstrong placed his boots on the surface of the moon and spoke those famous words, "That's one small step for man, one giant leap for mankind."

Charles Garfield was a young computer programmer who worked on the Apollo 11 mission. In his book *Peak Performers,* he speaks of how for the first time he witnessed people exercising exceptional levels of personal performance. Inspired by the challenge to put a man on the moon, people constantly performed "at the height of their abilities and produced at amazing levels".[12] However, once the mission was accomplished, those same levels of performance soon dissipated. Everyone needs a "man-on-the-moon-mission" to motivate them – a drumbeat heard above and beneath the cacophony in modern society.

EVERYONE NEEDS A MAN-ON-THE-MOON MISSION TO MOTIVATE THEM

Robert Kriegel researched over 500 peak performers involved in business, the arts, and sport. He stated that "no two were alike,

12 Charles Garfield, *Peak Performers* (William Morrow & Company Ltd, 1986)

but the one quality they had in common was passion! It was their drive, enthusiasm and desire that distinguished them".[13] Passionate people are self-starters; as John Maxwell puts it, they "never have to push [themselves] to start, [although they] may have to force [themselves] to stop".[14] With a clear understanding of God's glorious intent for humanity, preachers are by calling big-picture people, but when the image fades, and the mission with it, the passion soon follows. Listless, lethargic preachers lose their spiritual vitality when they no longer walk in the goodness of ongoing revelation. *"If people can't see what God is doing, they stumble all over themselves, but when they attend to what he reveals, they are most blessed."*[15] Without the *spirit of wisdom and of revelation in the knowledge of Him,*[16] a preacher will become lifeless and undisciplined. To maintain the fire of God within we need to find people, objects, and events that stoke our furnaces. Just as the dead man in 2 Kings 13:21 came alive when his body touched the bones of Elisha, we need to be touched by the hand of God in prayer

---

A PURPOSE IN LIFE WILL CREATE A PASSION THAT LEADS TO OUTSTANDING PERFORMANCE LEVELS

---

13 John Maxwell, *Passion – Turning a Burning Ember into a Roaring Fire* Vol. 10, No. 5 (Injoy Life Club, 1994)
14 John Maxwell, Passion
15 Proverbs 29:18, MSG
16 Ephesians 1:17, NASB

and experience the resurrection life of fire-lighting events, people, talks, books, etc.[17]

Second Nature

Sadly, the missing element in so much of what masquerades as present-day preaching is a lack of spiritual passion. This, for Christ followers, is a total anomaly because, through the redemptive, regenerating work of the Holy Spirit, we have become *partakers of the divine nature.*[18] What is it about God's nature that should become part of our human nature too? When we are born again and filled with the Holy Spirit, we should become passionate. Why? Because God Himself is passionate. Consider what A.W. Tozer says:

"GOD DWELLS IN A STATE OF PERPETUAL ENTHUSIASM."

"God dwells in a state of perpetual enthusiasm. He is delighted with all that is good and lovingly concerned about all that is wrong. He pursues His labours always in a fullness of holy zeal . . . Whatever else happened at Pentecost, one thing that cannot be missed by the most casual observer was the sudden upsurging of moral enthusiasm. Those first disciples burned with

[17] Romans 8:11
[18] 2 Peter 1:4, KJV

a steady, inward fire. They were enthusiastic to the point of complete abandon."[19]

It should be no surprise to learn that John Wesley, when his heart was strangely warmed in 1738, became a man filled with revival fire. He and his followers were accused of being "enthusiasts" – not a polite term in those days!

GODLY PREACHERS ARE SUPERNATURALLY INVESTED WITH A VIBRANT PASSION TO SHARE THE GOSPEL OF THE KINGDOM

With an ever-growing knowledge of God's eternal plan (the Word) and the infilling of God's power (the Spirit), preachers are supernaturally invested with a vibrant passion to share the Good News of the kingdom. This does not mean over-the-top charismatic circus acts. It means being empty of self and full of God's Spirit.

This is the godly passion that characterised the life of Jesus and it was clearly overwhelming at times for those who met Him. For example, Jesus did not preach a polite message when He entered the Temple. He upset the religious, overturned a consumeristic culture, and set about restoring the true purpose for His Father's house. Observing this volcanic eruption, the disciples recalled the words

19 A.W. Tozer, *Of God and Men* (WingSpread Publishers, 2015)

of the psalmist, *zeal for your house will consume me.*[20] Like a spiritual tsunami, Jesus' passion swept aside religious compromise to restore the purpose of heaven on earth. Likewise, knowing *the kingdom of God is not a matter of rules . . . but is in the realm of the Holy Spirit, filled with righteousness, peace, and joy,*[21] the best preachers are those passionate about the redemption and restoration of mankind. Preaching is therefore not some voluntary pastime, an optional extra we attach to our secular career, a hobby we do in our spare time; it is for those *called according to His purpose.*[22] Although a post-Christian society might prefer preachers to present a thematic chat with little biblical content, anointed preachers boldly proclaim with the apostle Paul, *we preach Christ crucified.*[23]

A TRANSFORMATIVE SERMON LEAVES THE LISTENER WITH NO MIDDLE GROUND

The purpose for which we are called is not to present a motivational pep talk but to present the all-sufficient life, death, burial, and resurrection of Jesus Christ. Although we might prefer a more people-pleasing, less in-your-face, softly-softly approach, this is not what God has called us to do. The ultimate purpose of preaching is

20 John 2:13-17, NASB; Psalms 11:1-18
21 Romans 14:17, TPT
22 Romans 8:28, NASB
23 1 Corinthians 1:23-31

that the listener will *become just like [Jesus]* so that ultimately they will be *co-glorified with [Him].*[24]

A preacher with passion will change a godless atmosphere. They will create an environment in which the Holy Spirit will convict and convince the listener, leaving them in no doubt that they will either accept the Good News[25] of the kingdom or reject it. A transformative sermon leaves the listener with no middle ground.

PREACHERS WHO ARE PASSIONATE ABOUT THE PURPOSES OF GOD ARE THOSE IN WHOM THE GOOD NEWS BURNS BRIGHTLY

Firebreaks

Firebreaks are created through human intervention. By removing combustible material, a barrier is formed that will either slow or stop a fire spreading. In both the natural and spiritual realm, without fuel a fire will die. If proof were needed, then the words of the risen Christ to the church at Ephesus bear witness to this fact. He declares, *You have abandoned the passionate love you had for me at the beginning.*[26]

Enthusiasm is an emotion that can ebb and flow, but in the case of these Ephesian believers it seems they had become overly familiar with the

24 Romans 8:29-30, TPT
25 Never be afraid of preaching the "simple gospel", it is a simple and powerful story.
26 Revelation 2:4, TPT

eternal by placing a priority on the temporal. This conflict of interests had caused them to abandon their first love. The remedy for this was to go back to their beginnings and experience a change of mind that led to a change of character – in other words, to repent.

Anything or anyone who dampens your enthusiasm for spiritual things or saps your energy should be avoided at all costs. Jesus had to deal with a group of fire-breakers commonly known as the Scribes and the Pharisees. He said, *[They appear] beautiful outward, but are within full of dead men's bones.*[27] Those who fight rather than feed your passion will drain you both physically and emotionally, leaving you vulnerable to attack. A negative person or environment, keeping late hours, a poor choice of reading material, lack of preparation can all serve to quench a preacher's enthusiasm. Beware of those things that seek to douse your spiritual fervour; preaching is a spiritual activity. We can block the flow of the Holy Spirit both in our preparation and presentation when we do the following:

BEWARE OF THOSE PEOPLE, OBJECTS, AND EVENTS THAT ENDEAVOUR TO EXTINGUISH THE FIRE OF GOD

[27] Matthew 23:27, KJV

- Try to be too clever or say too much
- Refuse to quietly wait on God in prayer
- Pervert the text
- Fail to be ourselves
- Step outside our measure of faith and anointing
- Let personal concerns get in the way
- Do not let the Holy Spirit master us in our preparation
- Allow the Holy Spirit to become the minor partner in our delivery

IN BOTH OUR PREPARATION AND PRESENTATION, WE NEED TO PRAYERFULLY ENGAGE WITH THE HOLY SPIRIT

Getting Engaged

To avoid self-reliance, we should remember that we are merely *common clay jars that carry this glorious treasure* of the knowledge of God.[28] We are fragile and easily broken earthen vessels that need the power and presence of God's Holy Spirit.

God poured out His Holy Spirit in Acts 2 to enable Christians to live a life that is naturally impossible. In verse four, we are told that *all of them were filled with the Holy*

[28] 2 Corinthians 4:6-7, TPT

Spirit and began to speak in other tongues as the Spirit enabled them.[29] In an act of obedience these Christ followers waited to be *clothed with power from on high.*[30] This shows that a daily engagement with the Holy Spirit is essential. As the Prince of Preachers once said, "A man who really has within him the inspiration of the Holy Ghost calling to preach, cannot help it – he must preach. As fire within his bones, so will that influence be, until it blazes forth. Friends may check him, foes criticise him, despisers sneer at him, the man is indomitable; he must preach if he has the call of heaven."[31]

From the very beginning, the Holy Spirit has been the guardian of God's Word. In the opening verses of Genesis 1, we find that the *earth was a soup of nothingness, a bottomless emptiness, an inky blackness.* Over this dark and desolate scene, *God's Spirit brooded like a bird above the watery abyss.*[32] Like some mother bird, the Holy Spirit waits to incubate God's spoken word. The Holy Spirit is given *that we may know the things freely given to us by God.*[33] Not wanting us to struggle as spiritual orphans, Jesus sent the person of the

WITHOUT THE TANGIBLE PRESENCE OF THE HOLY SPIRIT, SPEAKERS LACK THE CORE DYNAMIC FOR POWER PREACHING

29 Acts 2:4
30 Luke 24:49, ESV
31 Charles Haddon Spurgeon – The Prince of Preachers
32 Genesis 1:2, MSG
33 1 Corinthians 2:12, NASB

Holy Spirit so that *He [would] guide [us] into all the truth*[34] and enable us to do this thing called preaching better.

READ FIRE-LIGHTING BOOKS, ATTEND FIRE-LIGHTING EVENTS, AND SPEND TIME WITH FIRE-LIGHTING PEOPLE

For those who sense a calling to preach, feeding the fire of godly enthusiasm is vital. Avoid at all costs anyone or anything that will seek to dampen or douse your spiritual fervour. Both in your preparation and presentation, learn to partner with the Holy Spirit. Be sure to maintain a healthy balance between the Word and the Spirit because preaching is a joint activity between heaven and earth in which we get the privilege to act as purveyors of God's presence and couriers of His life-changing truth.

[34] John 16:13, NASB

Discussion Points

- What do you do to feed your fire?

- What are the things most likely to dampen your enthusiasm?

- What is the "man-on-the-moon" mission in your life?

10 ORDER A TAKEAWAY

Although a born-and-bred Englishman, I am a casual follower rather than an ardent fan of the beautiful game of football ("soccer", if you're from the USA). In fact, I can count the number of football league matches I've attended on one hand. That said, there is one international football match that has lingered in my memory for the last fifty-five years.

In the Summer of 1966, along with some teenage friends, I found myself in the seaside resort of Newquay in the county of Cornwall. Although not our normal practice, we had on this Saturday found ourselves in one of the local pubs. The date was 30th July 1966, and this was one of the hostelries that had a television available for public view. In the mid-sixties this was something of a rarity. While the Cornish cider was good, we were there for one reason only: to watch the 1966 FIFA World Cup Final.

This historic football match was being played by two old sporting rivals – Germany and England. The final was memorable not only for Geoff Hurst's hat-trick, but for Nobby Stiles' toothless celebratory dance around Wembley Stadium in front of tens of thousands of delirious England fans after the game was won 4–2.

ALTHOUGH THE PREACHER CONCLUDES HIS WORD THE HOLY SPIRIT CONTINUES HIS WORK

The 1966 World Cup was the first and, to-date, the only one England has either hosted or won. Going down in British football history, the final is also remembered for Kenneth Wolstenholme's television commentary. In the final minutes of extra time, when England had scored a third goal, he shouted, "Some people are on the pitch! They think it's all over!" A moment later, Geoff Hurst scored the fourth goal. Wolstenholme jubilantly completed his sentence with the immortal words, "It is now!" Kenneth Wolstenholme will always be remembered for those words. In the English mind, they are as ingrained as Neil Armstrong's when he landed on the moon.

When preachers conclude their sermons, they add a final prayer and people begin to leave the room. They wrongly think it's all over! But it isn't. The sermon may signal the moment when the meeting ends, but it is when the service really begins. The word that the preacher has brought now needs to be imbedded in the daily lives of the listeners – in the home, school, college, street, and workplace.

TOO MANY WELL-CRAFTED SERMONS ARE LOST WITHIN HOURS OF BEING SPOKEN

The best preachers reinforce this by working hard on creating a "Takeaway". They ask, "What will the listener take from my message into their week? Will this talk be relatable to their situation?" There are many reasons why this happens – personal resistance, fear, wrong choices – but when it does, declared truth can quickly dissipate. A sermon needs to be received in a way that has short-term encouragement along with long-term engagement.

Believing and Receiving

The New Testament word translated "receive"[1] is like a two-sided coin. In God's mind, there is both a passive and active dimension. You might

[1] The Greek word is *lambano* meaning "to receive"

be sitting at home knowing a friend promised to call. Hearing a knock at your front door, you realise they have arrived. It's one thing to accept the truth that your friend is waiting and wanting to come in; this is a *passive* response. It is another for you to get up, go to the front door, and give your friend access to your home. This is an *active* response. When James says *in humility* ***receive*** *the word implanted, which is able to save your souls,*[2] he is thinking of both the passive and active dimensions.

TRANSFORMATION HAPPENS WHEN LISTENERS APPROPRIATE BIBLICAL TRUTH

When you preach a message, those that listen to you might passively accept that the Word of God is seeking to gain access to their lives. They might even mentally acknowledge the transforming power inherently present in God's Word. But they still need to actively decide to open their lives and give the truth access. They need to receive in both the active as well as the passive sense.

We may love the fact that people seem to be accepting the words we are delivering with their smiling faces, nods of agreement, even some encouraging words (although

[2] James 1:21, NASB

the latter perhaps not in the United Kingdom!). But while all this is admirable, it's not over!

Having spoken your concluding words, it is with relief you take your seat. The hours of preparation have, by God's grace, enabled you to deliver the burden of your message. Like some musical symphony, the climactic crescendo has created an atmosphere of joyful excitement. The listeners have sounded a non-verbal "Amen". Relieved that you managed to complete the task without any major mistakes, you hand back to the leader. As you sit down you may think that it is all over – but you're wrong! You may have sown seeds of truth, but the growth of those seeds now needs to happen. The sad thing is that there are four kinds of responses, at least as far as Jesus' Parable of the Sower is concerned. These are all examples of *receiving* God's Word. One is positive. Three are negative.

A PUBLIC RESPONSE FOR PRAYER CAN BE A MOMENTARY EXPERIENCE THAT IS EASILY LOST OR FORGOTTEN

Firstly, some seeds fall on fertile ground which over the coming hours will germinate and produce fruit.[3] This represents listeners who hear the Word of God and receive it both actively as well as passively.

[3] 1 Corinthians 3:7

They let it take root and grow in their lives. Secondly, other seeds will have fallen on *the beaten path.* This represents *the heart of the one who hears . . . but doesn't understand it.* Thirdly, other seed falls on stony ground or gravel, symbolising those who shortly after they hear it, allow *trouble and persecutions* to prevent *the truth sinking deeply into [their] heart[s].* Finally, there are those in whom the seed is *sown among weeds.* The weeds symbolise *all of life's busy distractions.* The listener's *divided heart, and his ambition for wealth, result in suffocating the kingdom message,* preventing him *from bearing spiritual fruit.*[4]

ALTHOUGH OUR PREACHING MIGHT BE ENGAGING, FASCINATING, AND CHALLENGING, IT MAY PRODUCE LITTLE BY WAY OF TRANSFORMATION

Whether we like it or not, all listeners have either a positive, negative, or neutral response to what they have just heard. Even though some may hold a brief discussion grading you on a 1 to 10 scale – 10 being the most impactful sermon they have ever heard – most people will have forgotten your sermon within hours. The ultimate proof that our preaching has been profitable is the *Monday Morning Test.* In what way will our listeners be challenged the next day

[4] Matthew 13:19-23, TPT

to outwork the word in their home, study, and work environment? Will their public commitment on a Sunday resonate with their private Monday activities? Will the bold promises they make to God survive beyond the exit door of the church?

Mirror Dynamics

The Bible likens itself to a *mirror, sword, fire, hammer, lamp, food,* and *seed.* These illustrate the lasting power and potential of God's Word. The Bible becomes these things in our personal experience only when we personally apply the truth we have read or heard in its pages. Like a suit of armour, the inherent potential is only experienced when it has been taken and worn.

JUST LISTENING TO A SERMON IS NOT SUFFICIENT; BIBLICAL TRUTH SEEKS APPLICATION

Imagine you are travelling in the slow lane of a motorway (freeway) and you decide to move out into the overtaking lane. Before taking any action, you will check for traffic in the rear-view mirror. For a driver to ignore what they have seen and attempt to move into a busy lane would be ludicrous. Yet, according to the apostle James, this is often the way people handle a preached word.

If you listen to the Word and don't live out the message you hear, you become like the person who looks in the mirror of the Word . . . You perceive how God sees you in the mirror of the Word, but then you go out and forget.[5]

WHEN THE LIGHTS GO ON AND PEOPLE APPLY WHAT THEY HAVE SEEN IN THE MIRROR OF GOD'S WORD, TRANSFORMATION BEGINS TO HAPPEN

All Scripture has the potential of reflecting to us the reality of our spiritual condition. Just nodding our heads or saying "Amen" is not enough to bring about long-lasting change. As James continues, *Don't fool yourself into thinking that you are a listener when you are anything but, letting the Word go in one ear and out the other. Act on what you hear! Those who hear and don't act are like those who glance in the mirror, walk away, and two minutes later have no idea who they are, what they look like.*[6]

The human mind has a natural tendency to become easily distracted. Within a few minutes of listening, we can lose the essence of what we have heard. Many great messages are lost during an after-church conversation, during the drive home, or over Sunday lunch. Someone may listen to a message on the truth that *my God will supply all your needs according to His riches in glory in Christ Jesus,*[7] only

[5] James 1:23-24, TPT
[6] James 1:22-24, MSG
[7] Philippians 4:19, NASB

to arrive home and find that the washing machine has leaked and there is a flood. The natural mind panics about the expense and in the worry takes its focus off the truth declared in the sermon that God is our sovereign provider.

The sparkle in people's eyes as you preach may or may not be a good indicator that they are buying into and building their lives upon the truth you are passionately sharing. By the time people leave the building they may have forgotten what you just said. How often has someone asked us about a Sunday message they missed?

"Oh, it was good," we reply.

"Anything else?"

"I don't remember. Sorry!"

Side-tracked by many pressing issues, the message that the preacher spent hours prayerfully preparing has been discarded in the carpark. Don't beat yourself up about this if you're the preacher! It's human nature.

WHEN THE TRUTH OF GOD'S WORD IS NOT GIVEN TIME TO TAKE ROOT, TRANSFORMATION CAN NEVER HAPPEN

In recent research carried out at the University of Iowa, James Bigelow (the lead author, and a UI graduate) discovered that "our memory for sounds is significantly worse than our memory for visual or tactile things. Ask yourself, can you remember that incredible thought you heard on the radio this morning? Can you remember what your partner asked you to do after work this evening? The chances are you will not. As it turns out, there is merit to the Chinese proverb, 'I hear, and I forget; I see, and I remember'."[8]

'I HEAR, AND I FORGET: I SEE, AND I REMEMBER'

Although we tend to think that the various parts of the brain all work together, Bigelow's research shows that our brains use separate pathways to process information. Verbal, visual, and tactile information is memorised differently. Amy Poremba concluded that, "As teachers, we want to assume students will remember everything we say. But if you really want something to be memorable you may need to include a visual or hands-on experience, in addition to auditory information."[9]

In other words, give your audience takeaways!

Reimagining Our Approach

In his *Experiential Storytelling,* Mark

[8] https:www.sciencedaily.com/releases/2014/02/140226174439.htm
[9] https:www.sciencedaily.com/releases/2014/02/140226174439.htm

Miller writes, "Old ways of communicating God's message simply don't hit the mark for today's postmodern generation. They want (and need) more than 3-point sermons and dry dialogue. What's needed is a radical approach to teaching and preaching the gospel – and who better to look to than the ultimate teacher, Jesus?" He goes on to state that people "want to be touched, not by the numbing effect of top-down monologue aimed at the mind, but by the power of a full-bodied experience".[10] This is true, but we need to remember that while Jesus used storytelling with the crowds, he used a more dialogical approach with religious people. That said, people today respond to stories, so we need to follow Jesus and re-learn the art of storytelling.

IN AN EVER-CHANGING WORLD WE NEED A RADICAL APPROACH TO PREACHING THE GOSPEL OF THE KINGDOM

Much to my own surprise, I recently rediscovered the power of story. Baiting the hook with a sermon title, "Lessons Learnt on a Ten-hour Flight to Dallas", I could see that people were engaged from the very beginning. For me, this was a wake-up call to remember the power of story, to enjoy the

10 Mark Miller, *Experiential Storytelling* (Zondervan, 2003)

excitement of finding new ways of telling the greatest story ever told. Perhaps now is the time to re-imagine our approach.

With the re-emergence of the creative arts in the church, Christianity has an opportunity to engage in developing new narratives, to think outside the box and try different ways of telling the gospel story. With wisdom and mentorship, preachers need to push past the accepted norms of a sermon. Maybe we have relied too much on being in the classroom when the rest of society is in the living room. Jesus was more "living room" when preaching to outsiders like the Gentiles or non-Jews. He used the classroom style when teaching insiders, those within the Jewish Synagogue and Temple, especially its leaders. In public, he used a more interactive, conversational, storytelling approach to proclaiming the truth. "Tell me and I forget, teach me and I may remember, involve me and I learn."[11]

JESUS WAS A DOCTRINAL DEBATER AS WELL AS A MASTER STORYTELLER.

Order the Takeaway

Whether we conclude our Sunday

[11] Mark Miller, *Experiential Storytelling*

message with an open-ended question or a public prayer, we need to consider what our listeners will take away so that they can more fully live out their faith. When they activate the truth, how will the listener become a better parent, husband, wife, teenager, single person, employee, employer, unemployed person, neighbour, or student? I cannot emphasise enough the importance of "takeaways". Whether with a question, altar call, or a public prayer, the preacher needs to earth biblical truth if the message is to land properly in people's lives. Here are some examples of takeaways from my own life.

LISTENERS NEED A *TAKE-AWAY* SO AS TO LIVE IN THE GOOD OF WHAT JESUS SAID

Last Supper

Having preached on the importance of the table in Eastern culture, I turned to the Last Supper and the power of the New Covenant as represented in the breaking of bread. The setting for this sermon – a church that met in a former theatre – made a takeaway easy. We had arranged for a version of Leonardo da Vinci's painting of the Last Supper to be lowered like a giant curtain. The reproduction of the original was stunning. In the closing to the sermon, people were encouraged to come forward and write prayers or personal causes for praise on Post-it notes and attach them to the painting. We then collected all the notes and read and prayed over them. Here you can clearly see that the listeners were encouraged not just to hear but to touch, see, etc.

DOES PREACHING NEED TO BE VISUAL AS WELL AS VOCAL?

Pebbles

I preached a sermon on how David took five smooth stones into the battle against Goliath. I said that he did not take five pebbles because he was a poor shot but because Goliath had four brothers and David was planning to kill all of them. Prior to the service, we had prepared small see-through drawstring bags in which we had placed five pebbles. At the end, when listeners came forward for prayer, we encouraged each person to take home one of these bags of pebbles and place them in a prominent position to remind them of the fact that in Christ we are overcomers.

Shoes

The hook in this sermon was very unusual. We employed two secular ballet dancers to perform to a selection of songs about putting on new shoes. The sermon was built around John 8:31-32 which I paraphrased as, "If you walk in the good of what Jesus says, you will know the truth and the truth will set you free." During the closing moments of the service, we encouraged people to come forward and write with large felt-tipped pen on the soles of their shoes, John 8:31-32, as a reminder through the week of the need to walk in the freedom of what Jesus brought.

INANIMATE OBJECTS CAN SOMETIMES HELP US LIVE IN THE GOOD OF WHAT JESUS SAYS

Keys

Easter and Christmas are always a great time to employ an illustrative sermon. At Easter, I spoke about the empty tomb and how it was a door for exiting the old life and entering the new. We offered a practical declaration of that truth. Having created a full-size door and frame, people were encouraged to walk through it. They were invited to write on Post-it notes their personal declaration of what they were leaving behind. When walking through the opening, they put their anonymous note on the door. We collected them and the leadership team prayed over each one. On the other side of the door, we placed baskets of old keys. People took one as a memory aid for what they had prayed for that Easter Sunday.

A TAKEAWAY IS NOT AN AFTERTHOUGHT BUT A PLANNED AND VITAL PART OF YOUR PREPARATION

In addition to these examples, I have given small-length scarlet cords as bookmarks after a sermon about Rahab. I have also created fridge magnet mirrors with statements about who we are in Christ to help Christians live daily in their new identity in Christ. These should not be viewed as gimmicks but rather a simple attempt to create a means by which people can assimilate the truth. In biblical terms, we are doing what the apostle Paul advocated. We are encouraging people to *put on the new self*[12] or *put on the full armour.*[13]

[12] Ephesians 4:24
[13] Ephesians 6:11

Discussion Points

- What does co-labouring with the Holy Spirit look like to you?

- How do you creatively engage your listeners?

- How do you use takeaways at the end of your talks?

CONCLUSION

In the movie *The Darkest Hour,* Winston Churchill faces a dilemma of gargantuan proportions; his choice is whether to surrender to Nazi Germany or to continue to fight. With the British Army surrounded on the beaches of Dunkirk and Europe overrun by Hitler's forces, Great Britain was on her knees. In the face of these adversities, Churchill managed to rally a discouraged Parliament and country. With oratorial genius, he roused a sleeping giant and engaged it in the battle of a lifetime.

In the final moments of the film, while there is a standing ovation after one of Winston Churchill's greatest speeches, someone in the gallery leans over to Lord Halifax, played by Stephen Dillan, and asks, "What just happened?" Halifax replies that Churchill has just mobilised the English language and sent it into battle. How we need Churchillian preachers today, men and women who will look beyond the immediate into God's ultimate and preach transformative truth that will *Make the Mummies Dance.*

I have a vision.

I see an army of would-be preachers rising to proclaim God's Word. Secure in their calling and being true to themselves, they will become a voice of the future, rather than an echo of the past.

Given the opportunity, I would love to travel back in time and talk to my 23-year-old self. It was 1969 and I was afraid of further public humiliation and the thought of returning to the pulpit sent shivers down my spine. Memories of the *God's Only Forgotten Son* fiasco had created an acute dose of preacher's panic. But my would-be preaching skills were once again about to be put up for public scrutiny. The term schedule had been posted on the college noticeboard and my name was there for all to see. Thoughts of having to stand in front of such an audience terrorised me.

Much to the surprise of my peers, I had been accepted as a student at a denominational Bible college. While others thought I had a future in the family business or a teacher training college, I now found myself unceremoniously pushed outside my comfort zone into a religious educational institution. If joining a forty-strong student body – all of whom seemed more worthy of the privilege than me – was not bad enough, I had now been entered into the gladiatorial games euphemistically known as being "on the block". Feelings of déjà-vu flooded my mind. It was as if I was watching a re-run of my senior school year when, much to my dismay, my games teacher had entered me into a heavy weight boxing championship. Fortunately, on that occasion I was able to avoid public humiliation as no weighty opponent could be found. But this was different; I had nowhere to hide.

On the Block

"On the block" was a euphemism for the twice-monthly religious services attended by the students, faculty, and a few local parishioners. The "sentence" was carried out in the main room of the large Victorian manor house of the college. Second-year students took great delight in describing the horrors that awaited first-year victims. Following some hymns and songs, a first- and second-year student would preach. As if the peering eyes and listening ears were not bad enough, the following week each would-be preacher would be summoned to the principal's office. There, he or she would receive a personal critique of their preaching content and delivery. All this combined to create the feeling of being on the block. This was public humiliation. That's what I thought, anyway.

To say my preparation was thorough would be a gross understatement! In my mind I had created, at least in note form, a preaching masterpiece. Somehow, somewhere I had created a habit of using alliteration – something the dictionary describes as "the occurrence of the same letter or sound at the beginning of, adjacent to, or closely connected with words". No matter how many points the sermon had, they all needed to begin with the same letter. In my warped thinking alliteration carried with it an air of brilliance. I had decided that a well-alliterated sermon would compensate for my lack of preaching experience.

How wrong can a person be!

The trouble was, I had overdosed on alliteration. Even though I cannot remember the subject matter, I can still visualise my structure: three main points, all alliterated. Each main point had three subpoints, all alliterated. If that was not sufficient, each subpoint had three further subpoints, all alliterated. I had mistakenly thought that my literary skills would dazzle the audience. Although round two in the realm of preaching was not a total failure, my "on the block" experience only drove me deeper into the grace of God.

While my friends, along with the college principal, somehow found enough encouraging words to build me up and create a desire to improve, the applause of other people has never been my motivation. The drive to do what I have been doing for the last fifty years is not to gain people's approval but to sense the pleasure of a loving heavenly Father who in His infinite wisdom first called me into the role and responsibility of proclaiming kingdom truth.

Note to Self

If I could sit with my 23-year-old self, I would draw on half a century of preaching experience and encourage him always to remember the following:

- It is God's *call* that gives you the authority to preach
- In your most threatened and insecure moments, it is God's approval that matters
- Remember you are unique and there will never be another you
- Don't mimic others; *Be Yourself*
- *Find Your Voice* and the audience will follow
- Understand that there are struggling individuals waiting to hear you
- Learn to relax in who you are in Christ
- Listen to the Holy Spirit's promptings and co-work with Him

By putting an old head on young shoulders, maybe the lessons I have learnt will help would-be preachers to become the best version of what God intended you to be. When all is said and done, all any of us want to be able to say is that, by God's grace, we made the mummies dance!

APPENDIX

Before you go, there are some more practical tips for would-be preachers that did not make it into my final chapters. They are nevertheless important, so here goes.

Fight the Fear

It is said that 75 per cent of people place the fear of public speaking above the fear of spiders, heights, and even death. Most preachers experience some level of nervousness. This is often rooted in an experience where we were either embarrassed or ridiculed. This causes us to believe the lie that "I'm going to blow it," "I don't really belong here," or "They're not going to like me." For those who suffer in this way, the words that God spoke to the prophet Jeremiah may prove comforting. *Do not be afraid of them, for I am with you to deliver you, declares the LORD.*[1] Remember, the call to preach is a heavenly endorsement.

Honour the Time

"5 minutes of boring is five minutes too long. 60 minutes of fascinating isn't nearly enough."[2] The ideal length of

---

1 Jeremiah 1:8, ESV

2 https://careynieuwhof.com/sermon-2-0-the-future-of-the-preaching-and-reaching-the-unchurched/

a sermon is an issue of much debate. But whatever the optimum length, the important issue is that we should never abuse the privilege by going on too long. Whether you feel that you have sufficient time to deliver your message is not the issue. Standing before any audience is a privilege, something we should not abuse. If for any reason your time slot is cut short, learn how to adjust your material accordingly. To go outside the parameters set by others is to disrespect the pulpit and the people who have invited you to speak. It would be better to be remembered for your depth than your length.

Finish on a High

The conclusion of any public speech is the crescendo, the culmination of an argument you have been building. Always leave your listeners with a decision made, rather than a doubt evoked. Work hard to finish your message with a memorable conclusion. People need to leave with an overwhelming sense of God's amazing grace and a determination to act on what they have heard – not to mention a wish that you had said more, not less.

Make Them Laugh

One of the most effective items in a preacher's toolbox is humour. Whereas truth appeals to the mind, humour appeals to the emotions. Humour can open a person's emotions to receive a difficult truth they might otherwise find difficult to embrace. However, pointless humour is nothing more than a comedy act. Although the source is unknown, this saying perfectly encapsulates the point: "If I introduce humour into a message, it is because people don't know what I am going to say, but I do – it is humour with a purpose. Just when they are at their most vulnerable, I come in underneath the laugh with a word."

Mind Your Mannerisms

Like humour, our mannerisms will either help or hinder the communication of biblical truth. How we present ourselves physically is important. Whether we like it or not, the way we look, says a lot about us. Too casual can create the impression that we don't take the task seriously, while being too formal can create the sense that we are stiff and starchy. Be careful with gestures. Some preachers are totally unaware that they overuse their hands. Be sensitive to the image you may be conveying through your clothes and demeanour.

Use the Right Words

Beware of trying to appear too clever by using words that few people will understand. A college lecturer took their teenage son into a preaching class. He then asked his teenage son if he fully understood what had been preached. Knowing the audience is crucial. In the time when most people read a newspaper, preachers were encouraged to use *tabloid* rather than *broadsheet* vocabulary. In other words, be clear and comprehensible. If your teenage son can't understand it, then change the vocabulary.

Watch Your Tone

Avoid being monotone; raise and lower your voice to fit the topic. For instance, you cannot preach about the love of God with a cold, disengaged voice. To speak of man's destiny will automatically require a tone of passion. A monotone voice means death to the listener. While some build to a high pitch in the first few seconds and stay there, others drone on, never altering their tone. Both are equally off-putting.

Keep Eye Contact

How will you know if you are connecting with your listeners unless you look at them? The eyes are the windows to the soul. If they are closed, that's not necessarily because they are spiritually drowsy. It might mean that you're being dull. Periodically scan the audience. Pray that the Holy Spirit will cause your message to hit the mark. However, as the old saying goes, "If after twenty minutes you have not struck oil, quit boring." Never judge a congregation by its lack of verbal or visual response. Some people look disengaged when they are really engrossed.

Avoid Distractions

It is important that you do not allow people, objects, or events to distract, provoke, or discourage you when you deliver a message. You have a burden of truth which you need to share with your listeners, so keep your eye on the goal. Sometimes you can become distracted from your goal by an overlong session of worship songs before your talk. Or the cold temperature of the room may start to divert your attention from the task. Keep focused. Don't let your mind wander. Be ready to preach when the moment arrives.

Maintain a Good Attitude

What your listeners have heard about you could either have a positive or negative attitude towards you. If people have had a good report about you they will be prepared to listen. If their image of you is poor, you will have an uphill climb.

Wherever you go you have an opportunity for a fresh start, so handle your time well. Be positive. Be focused. And, after your talk, be available to talk to people, to answer their questions, and pray with them. Remember, we are not professional speakers who fly in and out of a meeting. Be humble, not aloof.

ABOUT THE AUTHOR

Chris Spicer is a preacher, teacher and storyteller who works with churches and Christian entrepreneurs. Chris has over fifty years of experience working with Christian communities and learning centres throughout Europe and North America. Having lived in Portland, Oregon, and Peoria, Illinois, Chris now lives in England where he helps lead a city-centre church. Chris and his wife Tina have four adult children and eight rock-star grandchildren.

Chris's other titles include *No Perfect Fathers Here, JJ and the Big Bend, The Reel Story,* and *Life on the Hill.* You can visit his website at www.spicersink.com and you can follow him on Twitter, Facebook and Instagram.

RECOMMENDED RESOURCES

Books

Timothy Keller, *Preaching: Communicating Faith in an Age of Scepticism* (Hodder & Stoughton, 2015).

Andy Stanley and Lane Jones, *Communicating For A Change* (Multnomah Books, 2006).

Carmine Gallo, *The Presentation Secrets of Steve Jobs* (McGraw Hill, 2010).

Dr Martyn Lloyd-Jones, *Preaching and Preachers* (Hodder & Stoughton, 1971).

Rob Parsons, *The Art of Communication* (Hodder & Stoughton, 2020).

Dave Stone, *Refining Your Style: Learning from Respected Communicators* (Group Publishing, 2004).

Chip Heath and Dan Heath, *Made to Stick: Why Some Ideas Take Hold and Others Come Unstuck* (Arrow Books, 2006).

Booklets

Mark Tanner, *How to Write a Good Sermon* (Grove Books, 2007).

Mark Tanner, *How to Preach a Good Sermon* (Grove Books, 2009).

www.ingramcontent.com/pod-product-compliance
Lightning Source LLC
Chambersburg PA
CBHW062100080426
42734CB00012B/2709

* 9 7 8 1 9 1 2 8 6 3 8 2 2 *